Compendium

Compendium

Management Cases from Emerging Markets

Dr. Anupama Rajesh
Prateek Mangal
Nirav Sahni

PARTRIDGE

To order additional copies of this book, contact
Partridge India
000 800 10062 62
orders.india@partridgepublishing.com

www.partridgepublishing.com/india

CONTENTS

MARKETING/DIGITAL MARKETING

HUMAN RESOURCES

PREFACE

The book "Compendium: Management Cases from Emerging Markets" is a result of my encounter with case writing at INSEAD, Paris and my sitting through a session of Professor Pierre Chandon, who talked extensively about the importance of Case Writing both as a pedagogical and an experiential learning tool.

Management Cases are an inseparable part of any Business School class. Cases help students understand complex business situations, apply theoretical knowledge and learn to articulate their opinions before any audience.

This book contains narrations of various business scenarios which require critical thinking and strategic decision making. They begin with the central problem and go on as an interesting story, culminating at a point which requires responses from its readers. They may talk of a fundamental business issue but are narrated in a suspenseful, stylised and exciting context.

The cases can be valuable to both students and instructors alike because one learns better when actively engaged. Tedious theoretical concepts are retained longer and understood better when they are applied to real life situations and discussed in classrooms extensively. These deliberations have an inherent benefit of honing their convincing and negotiation skills and developing communication capabilities. Case discussions and presentations also develop team building and inter-personal skills.

This book is result of the best wishes and blessings of several friends and my family. I express gratitude to my "Guru" (Teacher), Prof.(Dr.) Sanjeev Bansal, Dean, Amity University, whose constant support and motivation helps me overcome all kinds of barriers. My heartfelt appreciation goes to my family for their unconditional love and support throughout my life; this book was simply impossible without them. I am indebted to my mother, Mrs. Kanta Paul – who has always been "the wind beneath my wings", my father A.L.Paul for his blessings, my husband Mr. Rajesh Kumar for his prayers and the delight of my life, Aryan.

I would like to thank my co-author Mr. Prateek Mangal, for his invaluable contribution in the production of the book. A special mention to Mr. Anik Sahani, Mr. Sanjay Sahani and Mr. Nirav Sahni without whom the book would not have been possible; Ms. Jasmine Khan, Ms. Arishima and Mr. Havish for their help.

I offer my deepest and sincere gratefulness to the Almighty for inspiring, guiding and helping me take all the tests of life.

Anupama

Dr. Anupama Rajesh

SECTION

Information Technology

CHAPTER 1

Indian Prime Minister Modi - Politics 2.0?

EXECUTIVE SUMMARY

This case explores the role of Web 2.0 tools in micro targeting significant portion of Indian vote bank and its consequent impact on Indian Prime Minister Narendra Modi's campaigns. The case further focuses on harnessing technological innovations like social networking and mobile media platforms for soliciting support. This case study puts political marketing in perspective for understanding and critical analysis. It also explores the possible disconnect between PM Narendra Modi and people of India even after the strategic utilisation of Web 2.0 tools in his political communication.

Keywords: Narendra Modi, BJP, India Elections, Social Media, Twitter, Facebook

DR. ANUPAMA RAJESH

Her qualifications include PhD in the area of Technology in Education, M.Phil. (IT), M.Phil. (Mgmt.), M.Ed., M.Sc. (IT), PGDCA, PGDBA. She has a teaching experience of about 20 years including international assignments which include a teaching stint at Singapore and training of Italian and French delegates and students. She has written more than 20 research papers and case studies for prestigious international journals and has three books and several book chapters to her credit. She is reviewer of renowned Sage and Emerald journals and is the Editor of "Anukriti" - The Amity Business School Magazine. Her research interests are Business Intelligence, Educational Technology, marketing analytics etc. while her teaching interests are Business Intelligence, E-Commerce, IT enabled processes.

She is Head – Training, Development & Consultancy, Area Head (IT) for Management and Head of the Executive MBA Programme at Amity Business School, Amity University, India.

She has recently won the ADMA Research Award. She has also been awarded "Shiksha Rattan Puruskar" by IIF Society and won the second "Best Paper Award" at IIM Ahmedabad. She recently presented a case study at INSEAD Paris. She also has a MOOC to her credit.

http://amitymooc.com/home/itm.php

"India has won! Good days are coming."

The tweet on May 16, 2014 - which created history by being the most re-tweeted tweet in the history of India, in a way epitomised Narendra Damodardas Modi's quest and final triumph to the top post of India.

Humble Beginnings

Born on 17th September 1950 at Vadnagar, Gujarat to a modest family, as a young boy the present Prime Minister had sold tea on railway platforms. Around 1965, doing the same chore to several train-loads of army personnel coming and going from the border may have sowed initial seeds of "Desh Bhakti" or love of the country in him. This probably was also the origins of "Chai pe Charcha" or "Discussion with Tea" series during his election campaign and eventually the famous tea diplomacy with Barack Obama, the President of the United States of America on January 25th, 2015 which saw several serious discussions including the nuclear deal happening between the two leaders.

For several years after he had left home he dabbled in politics and social service, slowly growing in the stature in local and state units, eventually becoming the Chief Minister(CM) of Gujarat in 2001 which he would remain till 2014 for four consecutive terms.[1]

Early Advantage

As early as 2005, when the internet was emerging, Narendra Modi realised the importance of this electronic medium and its power to communicate and created the domain NarendraModi.in which went on to become 6188th most visited website in the World and 296th most visited website in India. He joined Facebook and Twitter in 2009. As a CM back in 2009 he showed a preference for e-governance, launching e-Gram initiative aiming to take technology to all parts of his state. He may well have been the first politician to use Google Hangout.

The Electronic Campaign

In his online "Thank you note" for his historic win on May 16, 2014 he rightfully attributes the social media for a large part for his win, crediting it for the connect established with people and their issues.

The study of his social media reach during electioneering is an interesting one.

The Year Before

India's then Prime Minister Dr. Manmohan Singh though a famed economist in his own right, beleaguered with corruption and policy paralysis charges against him and was a reticent man. His failure to communicate either in the online and offline mediums contributed to the drubbing that his party, the Indian National Congress will eventually get in the National Elections held in 2014.

---

[1]   http://www.narendramodi.in/categories/timeline

On the other hand the electoral approach of PM Modi's party was a strategic mix of digital marketing, content management and public relations to create an environment of positivity around the party. Vinit Goenka, the national convener of the Bhartiya Janta Party's (BJP) IT Unit and Arvind Gupta, Head of IT, charted out a winning strategy to complement Modi's already larger than life persona. They made him "visible everywhere" online using all possible tools such as Twitter, Facebook, YouTube, Google Hangouts etc. The "digital operation centre" was operated by youngsters who were supported by an online "army" of volunteers who kept retweeting and commenting actively making it almost the social media frontier. They acted as invaluable brand managers. With 280 million internet users which forms about one fourth of India's population, skewed on the urban and young, this was part of a strategy to win a historic mandate. BJP saw the youth as their harness-able vote bank and decided to play as per their needs, targeting this brigade with jobs, security and renewed hope. With 814.5 million eligible voters this was viewed as the largest election ever held in the world.

Social Media Platforms influenced about 30-40% seats and it was given its due importance in the campaign and resultantly in places it overtook the traditional media in its reach. Realising that social media was not just frivolities but a lot of people talking serious issues and agenda, all possible platforms were used as pillars to the edifice of electronic campaigning which would follow. Narendra Modi's presence was ensured in all electronic platforms including not so popular ones such as Pinterest, Tumblr, Flickr and StumbleUpon apart from popular ones such as Facebook, Twitter, YouTube etc. where he had amassed a huge following. The strategy was simple - to leverage the already very popular Modi, to constantly highlight the ruling party's failures and to raise the hopes of the disenchanted public. Very catchy slogans "Abki Baar Modi Sarkaar" (This time Modi Government.) and "Acche Din Aane Walen Hain" (Good days are coming.) were coined to cater to the moods of the nation and were disseminated by all electronic platforms and even ringtones! A unique combination of crowdsourcing and outreach was used. Many ideas were tossed in the public domain and ideas were elicited from the eligible voters to shape their strategy. Even the manifesto incorporated several suggestions of Modi's followers. An interesting concept of "organise online to assist offline" was used to recruit 2.2 million volunteers who like an army helped win this digital war. Key messages and relevant talking points would chart out the agenda of discussion for the online media.

THE SOCIAL MEDIA PLATFORM

The social media platform which was an important part of the overall strategy was used in every possible manner: to engage with voters, to disseminate vision of the party, information about candidates, local issues, ruling party's failure and BJP's narrative. This would take Narendra Modi as the most mentioned politician on Social media in India.

THE OFFICIAL WEBSITE

BJP's India 272+ channel portal was the initiation – it was designed as a communication platform to help the volunteers contribute ideas, collaborate and campaign. It consisted of extremely useful information about poll booths, booth officers and concerned voters which helped them target individual voters and garner votes. This "booth management" helped extensively in winning the elections. Detailed calendar of rallies and events enlisting venues and timings was made available. The e-book section had downloadable books laying out the vision of Mr. Modi and his party. It had an estimated traffic of about 9, 14,000 users.

TWITTER

A conscious effort was made to have real conversations and posting of interesting content ensured engagement. He had about 3.5 million followers then and each of his tweets retweeted abundantly. His tweets mostly centred on his campaign as he criss-crossed the nation, highlighting problems and targeting local and national adversaries. Of course deriding his opponents was also part of the larger plan of highlighting the present government's failures. This was also a powerful medium to dispense information about his rallies and sometimes give live updates. The pictures and tweets shared would be empathetic and sensitive to try to foster an emotional bond with the followers. The BJP4India twitter handle complimented and compounded the reach.

FACEBOOK

Again he had amassed a huge following, communicating his election travails. There would be rally schedules, agenda, important speeches and even live updates. His postings also included party's growth plans for the future of India and the failings of the outgoing party. There were also audio/video testimonials of his followers. Occasionally there would be greetings for various festivals or tributes to past icons. These were mostly in English and very few in Hindi despite many of the comments on his page being in Hindi – the Indian language. An interesting feature was contests such as "Mere Sapnon ka Bharat" (India of my dreams.) where the contestants had to upload recording of their vision for India. The Facebook page also had links to the app for donation. He had an engagement of 2.35 million leaving behind his all his rivals miles behind.

YouTube

At 1.32 million subscribers and a cumulative video count of more than 15 million the channel had a comprehensive cache of his speeches. There have been more than 120 million views of the various resources. All his rallies were covered and shared, and later embedded in his blog to cascade it further on Facebook and Twitter. A novel and commendable feature was to put vernacular subtitles to increase understanding. There were also inspiring speeches or messages by other party leaders, press conferences, even Q&A sessions. Sometimes there were clarion calls to join rallies or other events to be hosted. Another useful feature was televised views of the party on various matters of importance. To keep the interest alive there were occasional spoofs, or videos on relevant social issues like women empowerment etc. Sometimes there were also requests for donation. Even the cover picture was a call to support BJP. This channel removed the lag of communication with traditional media and kept the subscribers suitably engaged. The aim was to connect to the populace on an emotional level.

TV Channel

BJP also launched a dedicated TV channel to stream rallies, campaigns, speeches etc. It often ran features on the glorious past and vision for the future. This was linked to Modi's website and YouTube channel to magnify the reach. It had during the election days 4.4 million likes and 90 thousand tweets.

Google Plus

His page had a sizable following of the content dished out with similar content and he was way ahead of his competitors with 1.3 million people.

Google Hangouts

The strategy was not to leave any stone unturned. Modi taking the lead of a hangout which he had almost pioneered in Indian political space was emulated by the likes of Arun Jaitley, Sushma Swaraj and other party functionaries.

"Chai pe Charcha"

Wearing his humble origins on his sleeve Modi launched this "Discussion over Tea" – a digital interfacing tool where he or his other senior party-men would have interactions with people collected near tea stalls all over the country.

Blogs

Several blogs laid out his vision for the progress of India so that the voters felt assured of intentions.

Pinterest

Little known platforms also had a modest following of his pins and shares of his campaign trails and his future-plans.

Mobile Applications

An interesting mobile app launched in January 2015 already has about 40,000 downloads with a rating of 4.5/5 on Android Play.

WhatsApp

The party used this popular messaging application effectively for augmenting its membership and garnering funds. Thus there was a uniform approach and strategy across all mediums. There was sharing of content to convey a unified vision. This seamless integration gave a cumulative effect and reiteration enhanced acceptability. Though the content was tailored to the target profile yet had uniformity of approach to the party's vision

SENTIMENT ANALYSIS

Several publications carried out his analysis of his electronic electioneering, with The Times of India and Economic Times leading in positive stories while a scathing article in the Economist "India Deserves Better than Modi" brought a lot of negative engagement.

THE COMPARISON

Of course some credit of Modi's win could also be given to the lackadaisical campaign style of the opposition or rather then ruling party which Modi trounced. Their young leader Rahul Gandhi seemed to be out of sync with the population of India whose median age was 26 years.

THE RESULTS

Narendra Modi's party the BJP won 282 seats out of 543 with 31% of the votes share. With 537 million people voting (a record breaking 66%), a large share being young, the elections were almost a celebration of democracy with selfies showing inked fingers (a proof of voting) splattering all interactions. By the time he was sworn in as the Prime Minister of India, the world's largest democracy, he already had 16 million likes on Facebook – the second highest for any politician and his tweets the sixth most followed amongst World Leaders. Twitter India reported statistics of 2 million tweets on the Election Day! With a total of about 58 million tweets from start of the elections to the victory day. Facebook reported 29 million people making 227 million interactions through posts, comments, shares and likes.

THE PRESENT

Population of netizens in India is equal to the total population of United States and the social outreach has not curbed even after the elections. BJP is well aware that this sizable community which is skewed on the young and urban is really the winning factor and needs to be placated. The social media initiative is to be blended with the running of the Government, aiming to have a dialogue with the citizens and resultant participative decision making. There were several portals which are used by the Government of India (GOI) as well as the Prime Minister himself. India's press had cosy relations with the aides of the leaders of the previous regime. They are now faced with a Prime Minister who decides his own medium and timings to communicate. He likes to bypass the traditional media and wants to communicate directly with the citizens. He admires the transparency and honesty of the social media which he uses aptly to dispense information.

Crowdsourcing was used by BJP to lay out its manifesto and is intended to help design policies too. All these media were designed to listen to the suggestions of the public, monitor the results of policies implemented and understand the reactions evoked to get instant feedback and course correction if necessary.

Sentiments are tracked and data for the netizen's reactions is used to analyse the impact of various policies and initiatives. Any adverse trend is moderated with suitable bites to turn around the discourse. For example the contentious Land Acquisition Policy which was facing flak, red flagged the government to change its narrative for the same.

Not only the Prime minister, all ministries have been instructed to constantly engage with the public through Facebook and Twitter handles.

TWITTPLOMACY

Narendra Modi already had a sizable number of followers to his personal account @narendramodi, which rose phenomenally after his taking over as the Prime Minister of India making him the second most followed political leader after the President of United States Barack Obama with 12 million followers. In his unique style it conveyed to be handled personally rather being managed. This handle is also used to service the official @PMOIndia account. He has used Twitter platform for a unique kind of diplomacy. He used this medium for salutations to world leaders, congratulatory messages and even invitations often using foreign or local languages to do so!

The case in point where he invited the President of United States of America Barack Obama for the Republic Day celebrations through a tweet giving a new turn to the Indo-US relations

The relations with neighbour Pakistan alternate between cordial and frigid. PM Modi using tweets to wish the Pakistan Cricket Team or even tweeting the agenda of his foreign secretary's visit as "strengthening of ties". Only recently he wished his Pakistani Counterpart a "Happy Ramadan" and announced release of Pakistani fishermen as a peace offering.

PM Modi joined the Chinese social networking site Weibo before his Chinese visit and amassed following of 33000 on it with his inaugural post of "Hello China!"

His mobile is put to good use in his foreign jaunts often clicking selfies with his adoring fans or taking photos of beautiful locales. Aligning with the trend of embracing new technologies, he was the first world leader to use Twitter Mirror that produces autographed selfies often used by rock stars etc. His visit to Seychelles was accompanied by his posting picturesque aerial pictures of the island.

From serious, his posts alternate to informal even taking the help of Bollywood songs for the same. For his favourite "Swachh Bharat Mission" (Clean India Campaign) he posted an animated video of his own self sweeping with a broom to the tunes of a Bollywood number.

His digital operation centre consisting of motley set of volunteers, party workers, technology experts ensure he is trending online by tweeting his interesting speeches and various other hashtags such as #ModiInFrance to generate interest and keep his persona alive. #ModiInAmerica was instrumental in generating interest in his America visit and was partially responsible for the huge crowd at Madison Square.

Similarly the electoral victories of his Russian, English and Japanese counterparts were also acknowledged with the help of his favourite medium. PM Shinzo Abe of Japan who follows only six people including his wife tweeted a "thank you" post along with a promise to continue his work with Modi and India. For PM Cameron of UK who had duplicated Modi's own slogan to woo the sizable Indian community "Abki Baar Cameron Sarkar", Modi's congratulatory tweet was on the same lines.

FACEBOOK

The Facebook followers doubled after his taking over office. In fact he even has a sizable number of America based followers, surpassing some of American politicians.

YouTube

Prime Minister's popular radio show "Mann ki Baat" (Words from the Heart) are regularly uploaded to increase outreach.

Conclusion

Modi in an interview to ANI (Asian News International) sums up his social media outreach. "Two way communication.... Not only for dissemination of information but constant engagement... for varied purposes ... such as e-learning with the help of videos... exploiting the power of social media for social purposes... extending help in times of need, in Nepal, Uttarakhand, in logistics, in carrying messages to loved ones."

Questions for Discussion

1. How did Mr. Modi use a combination of various social media platforms effectively?
2. What are the possible risks of using social media to such a large extent?
3. What are the steps Mr. Modi will need to take to ensure he continues his success on social media?
4. Going forward, what are the ways in which Mr. Modi can combine traditional media and social media for maximum effect?

REFERENCES

Das, A. (2014, May 17). *How "likes" bring votes—Narendra Modi's campaign on Facebook.*
Retrieved September 26, 2015, from
http://qz.com/210639/how-likes-bring-votes-narendra-modis-campaign-on-facebook/

Mandhana, N. (2015, May 6). *How India's Narendra Modi Became a Social Media #Superstar.* Retrieved December 11, 2015, from
http://www.wsj.com/articles/indias-prime-minister-a-hit-on-social-media-1430905148

Pandey, V. (2015, 26 May). *Narendra Modi: India's 'social media' PM.*
Retrieved January 25, 2016, from
http://www.bbc.com/news/world-asia-india-32874568

PM Narendra Modi is second-most popular world leader on Facebook: Study. (2016, 18 January). Retrieved January 25, 2016, from
http://timesofindia.indiatimes.com/tech/social/PM-Narendra-Modi-is-second-most-popular-world-leader-on-Facebook-Study/articleshow/50624243.cms

Shenoy, D. (2016, 18 January). *NSEL: The 5,500-crore Scam No One Wants to Deal With.*
Retrieved October 29, 2015, from
http://capitalmind.in/2013/09/NSEL-the-5500-crore-scam-no-one-wants-to-deal-with/

The Big Secret behind Narendra Modi's Win. (n.d.).
Retrieved January 25, 2016, from
http://blog.venturesity.com/the-big-secret-behind-narendra-modis-win

CHAPTER 2

Acceptance of Change – The Postal Life Insurance Story

EXECUTIVE SUMMARY

Postal Life Insurance (PLI) is the oldest life insurance company in the country with more than 6 million policies in Postal Life Insurance and 22.5 million policies in Rural PLI making it the second largest insurance company in terms of number of policies. PLI is facing stiff competition with the other insurance companies as they offer wide variety of products and better customer services. To increase the market share and sustainability by providing world class customer services, PLI needs to equip itself with modern IT tools and techniques; this lead to the implementation of 'Core Insurance Solution' which will enable PLI to provide better customer services and operational efficiency. However, after the implementation of the solution in the Pilot phase, PLI faced lot of technical and functional challenges which are required to be resolved in order achieve the intended objectives of the IT project. The technical challenges will be taken care by the vendor however, the functional challenges needs to be carefully handled by the organisation itself.

Keywords: Role Mapping, Gaps in Training, Operational efficiencies, Acceptance of Solution, Change Management, Processes.

ABHISHEK GUPTA

Abhishek Gupta is Project Management Consultant with National Institute for Smart Government (NISG). He has 17+ years of experience in IT Project Management, Partner (Vendor) Management and Operations management providing strategic and pragmatic IT advisory and consultancy services to private and public enterprises and organizations. As a Project Management Consultant, he is responsible for planning, execution and managing the project schedule and timelines, quality of the project deliveries, address bottlenecks to meet critical project milestones. He has conducted various project workshops for managing stakeholder expectations and information sharing to ensure smooth implementation of the project.

Abhishek is Management Graduate (MBA) in International Business from Indian Institute of Foreign Trade (IIFT), New Delhi. He is an engineering graduate in Electronics & Communications from Kurukshetra University. He is a certified Project Management Professional (PMP) from PMI, USA.

SETTING THE STAGE

Even though the business of Postal Life Insurance was growing substantially but it was facing challenges due to increased demand of efficient and effective customer services and competition from other insurance players. Information Technology can enable PLI to equip itself with requisite modern tools and technologies to improve upon the operational efficiencies and customer services. With the help of technology upgradation PLI tends to achieve the following objectives:

1. To reach out to the wider population by introducing more channels for interactions with the customers
2. To develop a fully integrated life insurance platform to enable efficient and cost effective service to existing and new customers
3. To improve the quality of service being offered to the customers
4. Business processes and support functions to be IT enabled
5. To achieve "financial inclusion" of the un-insured rural population, while minimizing the cost of operations

ORGANIZATION BACKGROUND

The Department of Posts (DoP) is in existence for more than 150 years with more than 1, 55,000 Post Offices across PAN India. It is the most geographically widespread postal network in the world. It has played a major role in providing communication to the citizens and socio-economic development of the country. The major services / products of Department of Posts are: delivering mails and parcels, Post office Saving Bank, Postal life insurance (PLI) and Rural Postal Life Insurance (RPLI), Money Transfer and providing retail services like bill collection, sale of forms, etc.

Postal Life Insurance (PLI) is oldest life insurer in the country which started in 1884 as a welfare scheme for the benefit of Postal employees. Later on it was extended for all the employees of Central Government, State Government, Defence personnel, Public Sector Undertakings, Nationalized Banks, Universities, local bodies etc. To provide insurance cover to the rural populace and to provide the benefits to the weaker section and women workers of the rural areas, Rural Postal Life Insurance (RPLI) was introduced in 1995 by the government. PLI is at second position after Life Insurance Corporation (LIC) in terms of number of policies but is having only 2% market share in terms of premium income.

Post liberalization of Insurance sector in 1999 and with a very limited clientele base (government and semi government employees and rural section) PLI and RPLI had to face a stiff competition from both public and private insurance companies in the country. The only advantage it had over the competitors was huge geographical reach and supporting infrastructure of the Department of Posts. Because of these advantages and lower operational costs (as the complete insurance business is being managed by the employees of DoP), the PLI and RPLI offers insurance cover at a lower premium and higher bonus than the other insurance companies. Therefore the various products of PLI and RPLI are very popular and doing extremely well specifically in the rural sector.

CURRENT CHALLENGES

PLI is facing intense competition from other insurance companies which have various products like ULIPs etc. while PLI is having only the basic life insurance products. PLI needs to launch new products and enhance the service levels as per the industry standards. Hence there is a need to completely overhaul the operations of PLI with respect to People, Processes, System and Infrastructure. The key areas of improvement are

1. People

   a. Only a few resources are allocated for core PLI operations. For the daily operations of PLI, there is a huge dependency on the shared resources.
   b. No specific Job specialization roles and responsibilities.
   c. Frequent Transfers-in and Transfer-out of employees in PLI operations. this impacts capacity building

2. Processes

   a. Most of the processes are manual which are dependent on physical movement of files.
   b. Policy related rules and regulations are not as per the current industry practices as amendments to these rules and regulations are not frequent.

3. System

   a. Lack basic functionalities.
   b. Integration gaps between various modules.
   c. Works only as a 'Data Entry System'.
   d. Has been customized as per the understandings of the Circles leading to variations in policy servicing from one circle to another circle.
   e. No proper training provided to the staff for understanding the system functionalities.

4. Infrastructure

   a. Hardware and software are maintained by third party outside the organization premises
   b. Issues in Network connectivity and quality

TECHNOLOGY CONCERNS

The legacy PLI application, which was implemented in 2008, lacked some basic functionality as per the current industry standards like

1. Capability of the system to scan and store the policy related documents
2. It was just a basic data entry system without a Workflow Management system which is based on rules defined for the process. No Roles and responsibilities defined in the system.
3. Customer information related Letters, sanctions etc. are generated manually instead of being generated by the system based on triggers defined by the system on happening of the event / activity.
4. System was open to frauds / over exposure since the Customer cannot be uniquely identified.
5. No Standard Rules based processes. The rules were subject to the interpretation / understanding of the end users.
6. Integration gaps between various functionalities like premium receipts and claim payments which lead to cumbersome processes.
7. Non-availability of policy servicing facility anywhere across PAN India. Policy needs to be transferred from one Circle to Another Circle on policy holders' movement
8. Manual processing of Incentives / Commissions to the agents which takes time and is prone to errors which lead to dissatisfaction of the agents.
9. MIS reporting is very basic and minimal which does not help in business planning.
10. Absence of various customer interaction channels like SMS, emails, call centre, IVR solution, web portal, agent portal etc.

PROJECT IMPLEMENTATION

As the legacy PLI application lacked the basic functionalities, Business Process Reengineering (BPR) exercise was carried out to achieve the objectives. 'As-Is' processes were studied and 'To-Be' processes were defined during this exercise. Accordingly the requirements were coined from these processes and the Core Insurance Solution was designed as per the requirements. The main benefits of the solution are:

BENEFITS TO CUSTOMER

1. Efficient Customer services: With the implementation of the IT solution, the premium collection, claim payments and various other service requests will be entered in the system directly for further processing by the system. This will bring efficiency and transparency in the whole process.
2. Automated Claims Settlement process: For the normal cases like maturity and survival claims, the claim settlement process will be automatically triggered by the system itself without waiting for the customer intimation. This will help in quick settlement of claims and the claim payments can be made as per the customers' preferences.

3. Anywhere Services: With the centralized system, the policy can be serviced anywhere across India. There is no need to transfer the policy from one circle to another circle
4. Customer Interaction Channels: Various interactions channels for policy services will be available with the customers like, SMS, emails, IVR, Call Centre web portal etc.

BENEFITS TO DEPARTMENT

1. Increased Sales Opportunities: With technology advancements, policy issuance and claims settlement will be faster and smooth. Thus leading to better customer services.
2. 360 degree Customer View: Allocation of unique customer ID to all the customers. This will provide 360 degree view of customers which will help the department in Cross selling and up selling of the various products.
3. Ease of Introduction of New products and rules – With the ease of development and configuration of the new product in the system, the products can be easily launched and old products can be quickly modified as per the statutory requirements.
4. Availability of Web Portal and Agent Portal will help customers and agents in getting any required information and forms related to the products available online.
5. Automated Agent Commission generation: System generated Commission and Incentive statements leading faster and accurate payments to the agents.
6. Availability of the information related to the potential customers in the system for business

It was decided to implement the 'Core Insurance Solution' in phased manner i.e. Pilot Phase, Phase 1 and Phase 2. However, after the completion of the implementation in Pilot Phase, PLI faced lot of challenges (both technical and functional) which had to be resolved before embarking the solution in remaining phases. The Technical challenges were being taken care by the vendor however, for the successful implementation of the solution, the functional challenges has to be taken care by the organisation itself. Some of the major challenges were

MAJOR FUNCTIONAL CHALLENGES FACING THE ORGANISATION

1. Acceptance of the solution in the field: The success of the project depends upon the acceptance of the change by the end users. Change is inevitable for any organisation to sustain in business. However, acceptance to change faces resistance as people have to come out of their comfort zones to accept the change. There is fear in the minds of the people that they will not be able perform in the new system.
2. Gaps in trainings: The training provisioned to the staff was more theoretical than practical. The trainings were more in the presentations format instead of hands on practical training. The look and feel of the product has greater impact on the minds of the customers / end users.
3. Issues in Training Environment Code: Training environment code could not be aligned with the production code due to frequent critical changes which are required to be deployed in production environment for the smooth functioning of the PLI daily operations. Due to this there were gaps in the training provisioned to the staff compared to processes in the production environment.

4.   Understanding of the personnel due changes in the process: With the introduction of some new processes and changes in the old processes in the system, there were gaps in the understanding of the staff in performing the activities as per the new defined processes. Due to changes in the process, there is increase in the effort at the entry level in the system like scan and store the policy related documents.

5.   Gaps in Role Mapping: There were gaps in the work performed by the users in the old system and the new system. Because of these gaps, the users were not able to correlate themselves with their roles mapped in the new system.

6.   Frequent transfers of staff: Due to the administrative decisions, there are frequent transfers in the department. Hence the new users take their own time to understand the system. This leads to delays in the understanding the system and also the new users will not be able to appreciate the system and encourage the other users for using the system.

SOLUTIONS AND RECOMMENDATIONS

1.   Conduct Workshops: Conducted various workshops at the Circle and Region level to understand the issues being faced by the users. Help them in clarifying the doubts related to the new processes and encourage them to use the system. Create a team of motivated staff members who will in turn help other members in accepting the system.

2.   Learnings Document: Prepare a list of Learnings during the workshops. The gaps identified during the workshops were listed out with the solution. The list should be a part of training content and shared with the staff before the commencement of the roll out at their locations. Any learnings attained during the new roll outs to be appended in the Learnings list thus making the document a live document.

3.   Completely revamped the trainings:

   a.   the Selection criteria for the users and ensure that the selection is as per the selection criteria

   b.   By introducing more practical training sessions allowing users to feel the system

      i.   Aligned the Training content with the roles of the users.
      ii.   Analysis of the feedback of training received from the training centres.
      iii. Created videos, job aids, FAQs, training manuals along with the help menu of the application and helpdesk. State wise SPOCs identified for preliminary examination of the issues faced in daily operations

4.   Setting the expectations Right: The project is about complete restructuring of the current processes, changes in the processes needs to be clarified with the help of identified Change Agents. These Change agents not only help in encouraging the staff for using the systems but also help in providing training and clarifications related to changes in roles and processes in the new system.

5. Role Mapping: Ensure that the persons identified for the training are the actual end users who will be working on the new system. Also ensure that the end users are not transferred in the near future to the other divisions / department of the organisation.

QUESTIONS FOR DISCUSSION

1. What are the operational challenges being faced by Postal Life Insurance?
2. How implementation of the IT solution can help Postal Life Insurance to enhance customer services and operational efficiency?
3. What are the critical factors for successful implementation and acceptance of the IT solution?
4. What parameters could have been monitored by the organization in order to avoid the challenges faced after implementation of Pilot Phase?
5. Suggest other alternative solutions that could have been adopted by the organization so that IT solution is accepted in field?

CHAPTER 3

Connect: Preparing for the Digital Future

EXECUTIVE SUMMARY

Harish Singh, the Chief Information Officer (CIO) of Connect Telecom, had a series of interactions with the Chief Executive Officer (CEO) and senior management of the company who had unequivocally expressed their dissatisfaction with the way department of Information Technology (IT) had been functioning. It was felt that IT had the potential of being a strategic partner rather than doing just operational activities. Harish Singh was asked to devise a strategic plan which would strengthen Connect Telecom's initiative of enhancing customer experience by leveraging the IT department.

Connect Telecom operated in the competitive telecommunications services industry which had slowed down after 5–7 years of explosive growth. It was clear that instead of trying to acquire new customers, Connect Telecom needed to retain the existing ones through superlative customer experience. With that intent, Connect Telecom had conducted a market research which revealed the shift taking place in customer behaviour and preferences. The research indicated that the customers were very active on social media and liked to carry out all their activities through mobile phones. It was evident that active participation of IT department was the only way to improve the customer experience through their continuous engagement with the company.

The case discusses the challenges that were faced by the CIO due to complex interplay of industry evolution and changing customer preferences, legacy IT infrastructure and architecture, obsolete skills of the IT team, emergence of digital technologies and the heightened expectations of the senior management.

Keywords: Digital Technologies, Customer Engagement, IT Architecture, IT Strategy, Information Technology Management, IT Transformation, Business and IT Alignment

MUDIT AGARWAL

Mudit is an accomplished professional in the field of Information Technology Management. Currently working with Tata Teleservices as Additional Vice President – IT, he has diverse experience in a mix of multinational and Indian organizations like Hindustan Unilever, Domino's Pizza and Bharti Airtel. During a career spanning twenty one years he has worked extensively on ERP, CRM, Data Warehouse and Business Intelligence, E-Commerce portal and sales force mobile applications. Mudit earned his Bachelor of Engineering (Electrical & Electronics) from Birla Institute of Technology, Ranchi and Post Graduate Diploma in Business Management (Finance and Information Systems) from the Indian Institute of Management, Lucknow. He has attended management development programmes at Indian School of Business, Hyderabad, Centre for Creative Leadership and Indian Institute of Management, Ahmedabad.

SETTING THE STAGE

Harish Singh, Chief Information Officer of Connect Telecom, stood near the window of his office and gazed outside while a thousand thoughts raced through his mind. He had a big challenge on hand. Connect Telecom's senior management had tasked him to create and implement an IT Strategic Plan which would help the company achieve its goal of enhancing customer experience. He was well aware of the internal and external environment and understood the IT related problems being faced by the company. He knew that the department had become bureaucratic and lacked innovation. Harish realized that he had to contend with the problem of transforming the IT department and ensure that it became more agile and responsive to business needs.

ORGANIZATION BACKGROUND

Connect Telecom was founded in 1994 when the Indian Government realized that the telecom sector needed a boost and the telecommunications department of the Government alone will not be able to drive it. Private players were invited to buy the telecom spectrum in various circles after which they provided mobile telephony services. Connect Telecom established a very strong brand during its journey of two decades which was appreciated by its customers. With the passage of time, it invested continually in the network to ensure high quality coverage across all towns and villages. Connect Telecom carved out the second position for itself in the industry in terms of number of subscribers. Connect Telecom belonged to a diversified business conglomerate which had started out as a family business. While the patriarch of the group, Ramkumar Gupta, laid the foundation of the group, his son Sushil Gupta was the Chairman and Managing Director of Connect Telecom. Sushil Gupta's education, BE in Computer Science from IIT, Roorkee and an MBA from Wharton, helped him develop an appreciation for technology related challenges.

Connect Telecom started its journey from Maharashtra circle offering only postpaid services. During that period mobile phones were expensive and not only outgoing but incoming calls were charged at hefty tariffs (average outgoing rate INR 16/min and incoming rate INR 6/min). Gradually, Connect Telecom expanded to cover the entire country (both urban and rural) and also launched prepaid services. Besides the basic voice services, data (internet), ringtones, mobile apps and other value added services had come into play and contributed approximately 35% of the overall revenue. Later on, incoming calls became free and tariffs dropped significantly (outgoing approximately INR 0.6/min).

At the end of the year (2014–15) Connect Telecom had a base of approximately 180 million subscribers and market share of roughly 19%. Connect Telecom's (2014–15) revenue turnover was INR 360 billion. The ratio of number of postpaid to prepaid subscribers hovered around 12:88 whereas the revenue ratio was 20:80. Data/Internet accounted for roughly 27% of the revenue. Connect Telecom's subscriber base growth is depicted in Table 1.

Table 1: Connect Telecom's Subscriber Base

Year	2003	2004	2005	2006	2007	2008	2009	2010	2011	2012	2013
Subscribers (million)	14	16	20	28	42	59	85	123	154	150	160

Connect Telecom was managed by CEO, Sandeep Verma, supported by a team of Corporate Functional Heads. Connect Telecom's countrywide operations were divided into four regions (each having a Regional Business Head) and 23 independent business units called circles, each having a Circle CEO who reported to the respective Regional Business Head. Circle CEOs were supported by a team of Circle Function Heads who had a matrix reporting relationship with the Corporate Function Heads. This structure is depicted in Figure 1.

Figure 1: Connect Telecom's Organisation Structure

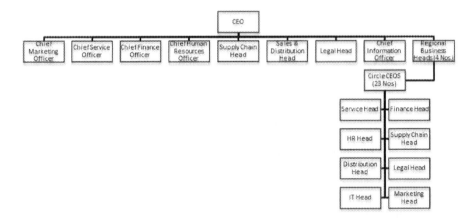

Connect Telecom had approximately 7000 employees with an average age of 33 years. Most of the employees, including the senior management were quite technology savvy and updated on the latest developments in the industry. Besides its own employees, Connect Telecom relied heavily on its partners in the areas of call centres for customer service and a network of distributors and channel partners for sales and distribution. Connect Telecom also ran its own branded outlets which were approximately 1800 in number.

THE MACRO ENVIRONMENT

Telecom industry customers had grown phenomenally between 2005 and 2010 as can be seen in Table 2. That was also the time when hyper competition led to price wars which resulted in poor financial condition of most telecom companies. Subsequently, the growth had tapered off and new subscribers were few to come by.

Table 2 (Source: World Bank)

Year	Number of Subscribers (million)	Growth over previous year (%)
2002	13.2	
2003	34.1	159.4
2004	53.0	55.1
2005	91.5	72.8
2006	168.8	84.4
2007	237.8	40.9
2008	353.5	48.7
2009	535.7	51.5
2010	768.0	43.4
2011	913.1	18.9
2012	883.5	-3.2
2013	905.7	2.5
2014	964.8	6.5

While the number of subscribers was not growing significantly, the industry had started to witness a shift from voice to data/internet as depicted in Table 3.

Table 3 (Source IAMAI and IMRB)

Time Period	Total Internet Users (million)	Mobile Internet Users (million)		
		Total	Rural	Urban
June 2012	137	48	4	44
June 2013	190	91	21	70
October 2013	205	110	25	85
June 2014	243	137	36	101
October 2014	278	159	40	119
December 2014	302	173	45	128
March 2015	330	192	49	143
June 2015	354	238	68	171
October 2015	375	276	80	197
December 2015	402	306	87	219
June 2016 (estimated)	462	371	109	262

Connect Telecom was not immune to this change taking place in the market. Slowly, the mobile phone was becoming the de facto device for connecting to the internet. Customers had started communicating more through instant messaging applications (WhatsApp, Viber etc.) rather than making calls or sending SMSs. This was also being fuelled by the easy and economical availability of smart phones. This shift had a bearing on the strategy that the service providers (including Connect Telecom) devised for engaging with the customers.

CASE DESCRIPTION - THE RESEARCH

It was imperative for Connect Telecom to revise its understanding of the customers in the new environment. Connect Telecom commissioned a market research to gain insights into the changed behaviour of mobile customers. The research findings made some startling revelations in the way customers' expectations had changed. It is indicated in the Table 4.

Table 4: Changes in Customer Expectations

Activity	The Old Way	The New Way
Who is in control of the conversation?	The organization - Whether it's an outbound marketing or an inbound call, the company can allot a predictable time	The customer - Communication is started with a public post which can invite more negative or positive posts and shares by other customers
What is the conversation based on?	Transaction - Companies try to sell or address complaints and queries	Interaction - Companies attempt to engage customers based on their interests, sentiments and trending social events or issues
Where does one get market insights?	Inside Out - Companies digs into internal data for analytics and tries to understand market trends, customer insights and sentiments	Outside In - Companies looks into the social media for the insights
Who is managing?	Customer Service - Typically the CRM is managed by the customer service for outbound and inbound communication	Marketing - A separate team handles the social media strategy to gain customer attention
Hours of Operation?	Fixed Hours - While the voice call centres are available 24/7, the email or chats are normally attended to during fixed hours	24/7 - Customers don't wait. They post anytime, anywhere and expect immediate response

Connect Telecom's Customer Service Head was witness to this changing behaviour. Customers were very vocal on social media platforms like Facebook, Twitter and WhatsApp. In case of any bad experience with the company they did not hesitate in posting it on these platforms and it quickly proliferated into collective online bashing.

Customers of Connect Telecom were loyal and appreciative of the services. A large percentage (approximately 60%) of these customers had stayed with Connect Telecom for years. Connect Telecom enjoyed the image of providing good quality network, honest billing and customer friendly support services. However, with the changing times, the demographics of these customers changed leading to changed expectations. These customers typically fell in the age group of (30–40) years. Around 30% of its customers were below 30 years of age and were the ones who had grown up with exposure to internet, social media and mobile telephony. These were also the customers who were well aware of the global trends. Connect Telecom realized that these customers were increasingly important to its future as they started to become a larger segment of its customer base.

On the basis of research findings and the fact that getting new customers was a challenge, retention of the existing customers was of paramount importance. IT was expected to play a key role in driving customer experience and engagement which were the main contributors to customer retention.

Connect Telecom's Information Technology Eco-System

Connect Telecom had always recognized the need for investments in information technology and over a period of time it had invested in multiple technology solutions.

In the year 2002, Connect Telecom decided to outsource the IT operations and delivery to a world renowned IT services company. Capital investment on IT capability was done by the partner and in turn Connect Telecom paid them a share of annual revenue. This model worked extremely well when there was exponential industry growth until the year (2012–13) (refer Table 2). Due to the legacy of working with large outsourced vendors, internal IT team Connect Telecom focused largely on vendor governance and project management.

Besides actual development and delivery, most of the technical architecture and design work was executed by the vendors with Connect Telecom's IT being the approving authority. Traditionally, a part of the corporate IT team was mapped to various business functions and supported these departments in their initiatives. They also managed relationships with their business counterparts and ensured that escalations were minimal. The corporate IT team acted as a bridge between the users and the outsourced partners and vendors. When Harish Singh (CIO) interacted with the IT team on joining the company, he realized that the skill level of this team needed an upgrade, either through training or through new hires.

Connect Telecom (through the outsourced partner) had set up its primary data centre (DC) in Mumbai and the disaster recovery data centre (DR-DC) in Noida. All its office locations (including outsourced call centres) were connected to the data centre over dedicated MPLS links with adequate fall back options. Distributors and Channel partners connected through internet. The branded stores were connected through a mix of dedicated links and broadband internet. Information security processes and controls were adequately in place.

The company had deployed leading business applications like ERP, CRM, Billing and Charging, Service Provisioning, Data warehouse and Business Intelligence (all essential to the functioning of a telecom service provider). These applications were integrated with each other through a common middleware. While the transaction systems took care of the operational processes, Business Intelligence solution could provide various analyses. A large amount of predefined static MIS was generated periodically. Connect Telecom had created a website to provide information on its offerings and it also allowed subscribers to raise complaints. All of this setup worked well for Connect Telecom in managing 'The Old Way' depicted in Table 4.

CONNECT TELECOM'S TECHNOLOGY CHALLENGES

Changes were taking place in the world of information technology. New Digital Technologies were on the horizon and were changing the way IT capabilities were being delivered to the business users. Emergence of Social Media, Mobile applications, deep analytics (big data) and cloud services were providing new opportunities to transform the capabilities and delivery mechanism. These technologies were no longer a privilege of large IT vendors.

A large number of small vendors had come up with specialization in niche mobile applications. These mobile applications provided a fantastic look and feel and deep functionalities which were always appreciated by the users. Coupled with this, these vendors were agile and very accommodative of customizations and changes that were asked for by their customers. This scenario was a pleasant change for the user departments of large companies who often had to contend with bureaucratic and slow-to-react large IT vendors. These vendors approached the various business users directly unlike in the past when IT vendors came through the IT department only.

Moreover, most of the capabilities offered by these vendors were provided through cloud setup which meant that the need for IT department's involvement was further diluted. Business functions reached out to IT department only in case of integration requirements with the existing applications or to validate the vendor credentials (which seemed more like ensuring compliance with organization processes).

Connect Telecom's senior management was aware that the way customer service and engagement was driven in the past would not work in future. Business and IT had to be aligned to the new realities of the market. Large scale transformations were needed for Connect Telecom to stay relevant. The board had asked Harish Singh to come up with an IT Strategic Plan addressing the challenges that lay before Connect Telecom and the senior management looked forward to his recommendations.

ACTION PLAN AND THE WAY FORWARD

Options that Harish Singh could consider:

1. Create an IT Roadmap for 3–5 years horizon. The roadmap should address the transition plan from legacy IT setup to future ready setup. Evaluate creating mobile applications, social media and big data analytics.
2. Restructure the IT function and bring in greater accountability and ownership of the team members.
3. Create engagement models for better alignment of IT department with the business functions thereby making the department more responsive and agile.
4. Review the IT architecture and align it with new standards.

5. Build technical capabilities within the IT function. Consider training the IT team members on new technologies.
6. Virtualization of the data centre set up. Setup a private or a hybrid cloud and virtualize the computing environment. That would provide flexibility in capacity management and would make IT deliveries faster.
7. Create an innovation vertical within the IT department which focuses on the emerging technologies and solutions.
8. Lastly, engage a consulting organization to help him drive the transformation agenda.

QUESTIONS FOR DISCUSSION

1. Should Harish Singh consider training the existing team members on new technologies or replace them by hiring from outside?
2. Should Connect continue to work with the existing IT vendor/partner or evaluate other vendors who specialize in specific areas?
3. What should be the organization structure of IT department to support the expectations of the company?
4. What should be the constituents of the IT Strategy to support Connect Telecom's initiatives on customer engagement and experience?
5. How can Harish Singh drive transformation from legacy IT setup to the digital era?

Section

Rural Management

CHAPTER 4

Anaemia: The Irony of Iron Deficiency

EXECUTIVE SUMMARY

Anaemia is a malady which affects developed and developing nations alike. A report by Times of India in April 2015 stated that 50% of pregnant women in India are anaemic, making it one of the leading causes of maternal mortality in the country. This silent killer goes unnoticed and weakens the body from within. Adolescent girls and women are majorly susceptible due to poor nutrition and blood loss during menstruation. Poor nutrition is majorly to blame as the diet of the girls and women is not sufficiently rich. Additionally India is a patriarchal society, predominantly as a practise in rural areas, women eat leftover food of the male members of the family making them further nutritionally deprived.

Ramvanti Devi was a simple, God fearing woman hailing from Rajpura Village in Bastar District of Chhattisgarh who came forward to fight the silent evil of anaemia in women. Losing her daughter to maternal mortality had broken her spirits but she had decided to fight the killer malady rather than suffer silently. Due to the lack of education and inadequate government action, it is not considered a life threatening condition or even a serious problem but many who have lost a mother, a wife, a daughter or a sister will disagree. It is not that the Government does not try; there are periodic distributions of 'Iron supplement pills' at schools and at Regional Medical Centres (RMC's) but there are still a lot of girls who do not attend schools or have access to regional medical centres. In many cases girls are married off at an early age and are exposed to teen pregnancies, thus compounding the ill effects of anaemia.

This case study is a study of Ramvanti Devi's fight against the usually ignored risk and her efforts to change the practices in rural India, viewed through the lens of Social Marketing.

Keywords: Anaemia, Social Marketing, Iron Deficiency, Maternal Mortality, Rural Healthcare

ROHIT KAWATRA

An entrepreneur with a knack of creativity, Rohit Kawatra has been donning many hats. Apart from having 6 years of work experience with corporates like Cognizant, Triton and his own startup, he has a prolific academic side. Lately Rohit had been teaching marketing at a Business School in NCR region. He is a full time post graduate from IIM Kozhikode, and a mechanical engineer from Amity School of Engineering and Technology Delhi. He has been a champion under National Scholarship Scheme and winner of many academic and music events. He still continues his quest of exploring art and passion.

PRATEEK MANGAL

Prateek works as the Director – Client Services for SSR Management Consultants Pvt. Ltd. An MBA from Indian Institute of Foreign Trade, Kolkata and International University in Geneva, Switzerland, he started his corporate journey with Triton Management Services and served the FMCG giant in Africa and India. He is widely travelled and experienced across Europe, Africa and Asia and has six year of experience in FMCG and Manufacturing Industry.

He has a passion to gather knowledge and is also a Diploma holder in Cyber Law from Asian School of Cyber Laws, Pune. He has also been part of numerous Conclaves and Symposiums and has presented and published research papers on key FMCG and Manufacturing issues.

SETTING THE STAGE

Kofi Annan former Secretary-General of United Nations said "There is no tool for development more effective than the empowerment of women". In the true sense, no one can empower women more than women themselves. This is what Miss Sujata Das believed in, and this is what Ramvanti had in mind at the onset of her fight with maternal mortalities due to Anaemia.

Sitting in the antechamber at her home, which also served as office of Shakti, an NGO focused on women rights and empowerment, Sujata was thinking about how her life has taken a shift from a wife to a social change catalyst. She was the one who inspired Ramvanti to fight her own battles, and supported her whenever she needed it. In the year 2010 they had an idea, which has helped a handful of women in Bastar to reduce iron deficiency. Now they wanted to make this concept widespread and acceptable in order to combat the problem holistically.

CASE DESCRIPTION

It was a sunny afternoon in 2006; Ramvanti had just completed cleaning the house where she worked as a housemaid. She had been working there for the last one year. Ever since she had to move from her village Rajpura, her days have been the same. But today wasn't going to be the same. She had a letter in her hand, which was telling the story of her daughter Rajni's death during pregnancy. This instantly took her mind back to Bastar and her happy little family.

Bastar, a district in southern Chhattisgarh bordering Odisha, possesses a blend of Tribal and Odia culture. It has 85% rural population with 1024 females per 1000 males ratio. Regular Naxal attacks and killings of males attribute majorly to this unexpectedly positive sex ratio. It is majorly inhabited by tribal people who constitute 60% of the population. Bastar district had a population of 1 million. Ramvanti Devi was a farmer's wife. Major part of her life was spent cooking or helping her husband Sudhram in paddy fields where he worked. Lately they had been getting support from their daughter Rajni (13) and son Pavan (10). Their wages were just about enough to cover their daily needs.

World Health Organization (WHO) has estimated that there are more than two billion anaemic people in the world. Since anaemia is a late indicator of deficiency of iron, the number of iron deficient people would be almost 2.5 times this figure. The estimated prevalence of anaemia in developing countries is shown in Exhibit 1, and the severity of the same in Exhibit 2. In Bastar too, anaemia claims hundreds of women's lives every year.

The women were not safe in this area, for they were under constant fear of being raped or molested by Naxalites or rebels. Ramvanti got her daughter married early for her safety like others in her village. She was married in a family in nearby district Kanker. The year 2004 had seen a huge Naxalite attack at Bastar which had disbanded many families. She had lost her husband Sudhram and son Pavan in this attack. She left Bastar along with few other families and migrated to some other district in Chhattisgarh. After struggling for more than a year, she met Sujata Das, a world renowned woman rights activist, who took her to Delhi in 2005 and gave her means to earn a livelihood. In this one year, she had learnt a lot about other women and their struggles. Sujata had taught her "The world is not fair. If you expect the world to be fair with you because you are fair, you're fooling yourself". Inspired, she had slowly become strong and able.

However, the news of her daughter's untimely demise was too much for her. She was completely broken and alone now, for she had lost all her family one by one. Sujata saw her in tears and knew something terrible had happened. Sujata and Ramvanti took the next train to visit Bastar and Kanker. For Sujata, a new journey had begun. For Ramvanti, the previous life was over.

They visited Rajni's in-laws, and spoke to them about her life after marriage. According to them, she was usually weak despite a normal diet. Her weakness intensified with her pregnancy and eventually her foetus succumbed to weakness, blood loss and labour pains. Efforts by the local doctors could not save Rajni who passed away shortly.

Sujata then understood that the symptoms and the food habits of the family indicated iron deficiency in their diet. She spoke to other families in the same village to realize that iron deficiency was quite common in these areas. Together the two women went to different parts of the district. Sujata was taken aback by the fact that women weren't even aware of it. They were severely anaemic during pregnancy and still no suitable steps had been taken. The diminutive efforts of government and local bodies had been in vain. Every year young women were dying of severe anaemia and Rajni was another victim of the same misfortune. This trip was a true eye opener for Sujata. She was now keen on finding a solution to this problem in a more effective way.

They returned to Delhi and after spending a long time in research, Sujata thought of something which could turn things around. She had read about the use of iron ingots while cooking for improving iron content in the food. This practice had been devised recently; the method was simple and convenient. One had to keep iron ingot in the vessel while boiling water which would later be used for cooking, or even directly while cooking food. When the iron ingots or un-tempered iron vessels were used, there was a need to add lemon or lime juice to boiling water to aid the release of iron. Although few households used iron vessels for cooking, they were ineffective. These vessels were tempered and could not release iron.

Sujata wanted to try and find out if this could really work in India, specifically in rural parts of India. She discussed it with Ramvanti, who now was ready to work day and night for this cause. Ramvanti wanted to be trained and equipped. She considered this as her own battle and started doing the ground work. She went back to Bastar, but this time it was a mission that she was on. She started meeting women and educating them about anaemia and its prevention.

Current Challenges

Ramvanti gave away iron ingots to few women for a pilot study. She had met hundreds of women in few months who were deficient in iron. Not many women were ready to modify their old methods of cooking despite the counselling and motivation by her. She realized that these ingots were rendered useless by the women. These ingots were soon flattened by the families and used as trowel for farming. Some were using it as shim for balancing or supporting vessels while cooking. In few other cases, they gave away the ingots to kids to play with. The women had earlier too failed to realise the importance of iron and folic acid tablets distributed by the government making the program ineffective.

The women were illiterate and poor. The families had no idea of rich diet for pregnant women and mothers. Sometimes they didn't even have enough for meals. Anaemia was least of their problems. It was a Naxalite area and hence the dangers related to life and livelihood were more important issues than to fight anaemia.

Considering all these factors, Ramvanti Devi had to find a solution which makes sure the women use these ingots the way they are prescribed. The solution was simple, but the efforts needed were humongous.

SOLUTIONS AND RECOMMENDATIONS

Ramvanti Devi knew the habits and lifestyle of these households. It wasn't easy to make these women use un-tempered iron pieces or vessels. The women had grown up learning the use of aluminium vessels for cooking; those few who used iron vessels were not experiencing the benefits as the vessels used were made of tempered iron that did not release bioavailable iron.

People found the hassle of using the ingots unnecessary and avoidable, there had to be an attribute which could give it instant acceptability. Few women who understood the concept of cooking with iron ingots and believed in her had already tried it and were getting visible results in a few months.

Most women did not understand it was for their own good. Hence there was the need of a conscious effort of Social Marketing. Social marketing is defined as using marketing principles and techniques for the welfare of people and the physical, social and economic environment in which they live. It is a set of activities carefully planned, with long-term approach towards changing human behaviour. So she was looking for something that could alter the behaviour and habits of these people for good, without causing much resistance.

She had long and repeated discussions with Sujata about the various options they could try. The following months involved a lot of trial and error to find the best solution. Initially they started promoting the use of non-tempered iron vessels, but it was completely rejected by households as aluminium vessels were lighter and cost effective.

She realized that there had to be a symbolic significance to these iron ingots. A religious symbol could be more acceptable. Ingots could be shaped like something women connected with. Since women are considered to bring prosperity, fulfilment and fertility to a family, the symbol had to bear the same attributes. She thought of a leaf, a rose flower, an elephant, tree, chakra (wheel), and many other things.

Sujata travelled to Bastar again for aiding and helping Ramvanti out of her troubles. Bastar had a tradition of handicrafts made of iron and there were several blacksmiths. After a few visits, they finalized a blacksmith for creating cast iron ingots in different shapes. They tried almost all of these in the district. A leaf lacked any connect and so did a flower and tree. These were again used as shim or as a toy. Elephant shaped ingot was considered inappropriate for putting in cooking vessels as the animal is a symbol for Hindu god Ganesha and the women started using it for worshipping. Chakra shaped ingots were used for ornamental purposes instead of cooking. They even tried getting ladles made of iron and gave them away to some families. These too were also rejected or used for different non-cooking purposes.

This area had majority religious ethnicity of Hinduism. She assumed that a "Kalash (Pot)" shaped ingots (Exhibit 3), can be something which symbolizes growth and prosperity and can be used in cooking vessels without hurting religious sentiments. Eventually they agreed on trying "Kalash" shaped ingots. They even had to convince a few priests in order to add religious significance to these ingots. They took those ingots and distributed to a few women with an instruction that this "Kalash" would improve prosperity and health when used while cooking food.

The religious context made these ingots much more acceptable and less used for other purposes. They started getting more ingots manufactured by local blacksmiths and later factories. Now there were more stories of women benefiting.

After this, Sujata brought some professionals to these two districts for monitoring haemoglobin levels of people in the area. In a couple of years, they could conclude significant improvement of the same and reduction in anaemic cases in these districts.

Now they know the solution, but to make it a nationwide concept, one needs to look at the bigger picture. This will require them to transcend political, religious, social, economic and other barriers.

QUESTIONS FOR DISCUSSION

1. Mention any Social Marketing Initiative that you have come across in your day to day life.
2. What steps should be taken to ensure the Government Programs regarding rural healthcare are implemented on ground level?
3. What other steps could Sujata and Ramvanti could take for eradication of Anaemia.
4. Discuss the ways in which women can be empowered in Rural India.

REFERENCES

Bentley, M.E., and Griffiths, P.L. (2003). The burden of anemia among women in India. *European Journal of Clinical Nutrition, 57,* 52-60.

Chhabra, A., Chandar, V., Singh, A., Gupta, A., Chandra, H., Gaur, S. (2014). A Study of Anemia in Hospitalized Children in a Tertiary Care Hospital in Northern India. *Journal of Biomedical and Pharmaceutical Research, 3(2),* 80-83.

Gerardo Alvarez-Uria, Praveen K. Naik, Manoranjan Midde, Pradeep S. Yalla, and Raghavakalyan Pakam
Prevalence and Severity of Anaemia Stratified by Age and Gender in Rural India
Retrieved Februrary 18, 2016 from
http://www.hindawi.com/journals/anemia/2014/176182/#B1

Understanding Livelihood Opportunities: Bastar District, Chhattisgarh. (n.d.). Retrieved January 2, 2015, from
https://www.nabard.org/Publication/Livelihood mapping in Bastar Chhattisgarh.pdf

ANNEXURE

Exhibit 1: Prevalence of Anaemia in Developing countries

Age group	Gender	Estimated anaemic population
<5 years	Both	39%
5-14 years	Both	48%
15-59 years	Women	42%
15-59 years	Men	30%
>60 years	Both	45%

Source: http://www.hindawi.com/journals/anemia/2014/176182/#B1

Exhibit 2: Prevalence of mild, moderate, and severe anaemia by age in males and females

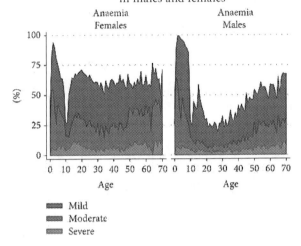

Prevalence of mild, moderate, and severe anaemia by age in males and females.

Source: http://www.hindawi.com/journals/anemia/2014/176182/#B1

Exhibit 3: Kalash design for iron ingots

CHAPTER 5

Water: A Drop of Light for Remote Un-electrified Villages

EXECUTIVE SUMMARY

In the Indian State of Assam, there are about 1600 un-electrified villages. Families in search of perennial water sources settle near small water streams and the settlement grows to become a village. One of these water streams is named as Langsomipi Nalla in District Karbi Anglong and its water can be used to generate electricity through Hydro Power Project[1]. There is a cluster of 8 villages consisting of about 160 households with a population of approximately 900 which do not have any access to electricity and these villages are spread in a radius of 4 km around this perennial water stream[2].

The planning of electrification of villages by putting up Micro hydel scheme[3] on Langosomipi Nalla was carried out by a team of hydro power engineers and it was found that a micro hydel scheme of installed capacity 80 Kilowatt (KW)[4] can be implemented which can provide electricity round the clock to each household (having 2 CFL bulbs and a Socket for Fan/TV), street lights, school, flour mill and dispensary in the un-electrified villages. This project could change the life of villagers forever.

There is a need to tap electricity potential of small perennial streams flowing alongside remote villages in the hilly regions of country by putting micro hydel schemes. This case highlights issues and the ways forward in the implementation of micro hydel schemes in rural India as these projects have a life of about 100 years and generate supply of power round the clock to the remote villages without any hazardous effect on the environment. Such infrastructure initiatives can bring a lot of cheer in the lives of rural folk as 24x7 supply of electricity can ensure the safety of women, better education for children as they can also study during night hours, updating of knowledge, entertainment through various kinds of media and better lifestyle.

Keywords: Decentralised Distributed Generation (DDG), Karbi Anglong, Langsomipi, Micro Hydel Scheme, Rural electrification, Un-electrified villages.

---

[1] Hydro Projects Classification – Projects running with River Water as source of energy. Large Hydro Projects have capacity >25 MW, Small hydro projects have capacity (0.1 MW to 25 MW) and Micro Hydel Projects <0.1 MW (100 KW). Hydro projects of less than 5 KW (0.005MW) capacity are termed as Pico hydel projects.

[2] Perennial River streams –Streams having some flow throughout the year.

[3] Refer Exhibit 1 to understand Micro Hydel Scheme

[4] 1 MW – Megawatt = 1000 Kilowatt and 1 electricity unit = 1 Kilowatt hour = 1kWh.

PARDEEP AGGARWAL

Pardeep is working with IL&FS Energy Development Company Limited as Vice President-Hydro. He is BE (Mechanical, 1993) from Punjab Engineering College, Chandigarh and MBA (Finance) from IMT, Ghaziabad. He has about 23 years of experience in project planning, development and implementation of small and medium hydro power projects. He has worked for projects located in most of the States of India and has surveyed projects in many continents like Europe, Africa, and Asia.

He has also worked in Water Treatment Projects, 12 MW Biomass project, Rooftop Solar Projects and 63 MW Coal Washery Thermal Project as Project In-Charge. He is also CEO of Assam Power Projects Development Company Ltd, APPDCL (a JV company of IL&FS and Govt. of Assam).

He has previously worked with Crompton Greaves, Snowy Mountains Engineering Corporation, Triveni Engineering and Industries. Mr. Aggarwal is member of various organizations like CBIP, Indian Water Resources and European Small Hydro Association.

SETTING THE STAGE

In an evening of January 2010, Mr. Adil Qureshi along with his team members was returning after taking care of some scheduled work in Karbi Anglong district in the State of Assam, India. On the way back, his vehicle broke down and it was not possible to arrange for alternative transportation and they were feeling helpless as darkness was setting in and it was getting chilly with each passing minute. Some Forest Officers on a patrol came to their rescue and helped them get accommodation in a nearby village Paplongso Biswanath. This was an un-electrified village and villagers were mostly dependent on kerosene for lighting their houses, though some of the villagers had solar lanterns too. As the night grew darker some villagers gathered and started having discussions around the bonfire which was their daily routine. Mr. Adil joined in and inquired about the source of water and the villagers confirmed that a stream called Longsomipi Nalla passes nearby. Being a hydro professional he advised them to start tapping the stream for power generation and informed them of the Government subsidy for Decentralised Distributed Generation (DDG)[5] scheme covering about 90% of the project cost. The people of the community were surprised and requested the team to visit the Longsomipi Nalla and nearby villages, the next morning. These villagers living in un-electrified villages face several challenges in their normal day-to-day life for example– safety of women as there is no street lighting, no fans, no education for children after sunset and fetching clean drinking water from far flung areas. However, some villagers use diesel for light but it causes lot of pollution though some of them have now started using solar lanterns but micro hydel schemes would be the ideal source of energy ensuring 24x7 electricity supply in these villages.

On their request, the following morning Mr. Adil and his colleagues visited the Longsomipi Nalla stream and took rough assessments of the potential of the stream and it was their view that the stream could generate enough power to supply to the surrounding un-electrified villages. After giving assurance of help to the villagers they left.

ORGANIZATIONAL BACKGROUND

The Government of Assam (GoA) is keen to develop the power potential of the State to improve its power generation capacity as well as the livelihood standards of the people. GoA understands that for speedy development of power projects, private capital is needed.

Assam Power Project Development Company Limited (APPDCL) is a Joint Venture Company of Government of Assam and IL&FS, having equal shareholding i.e. 50:50. APPDCL intends to identify, develop and allot power projects in the State of Assam to Independent Power producers on Public Private Partnership (PPP) format.

A beginning in developing Small Hydro Power Projects has already been made by APPDCL since its inception in 2007. APPDCL has successfully developed and allotted

---

[5] Off –Grid (Decentralized Distributed Generation) – The electricity produced is generally fed to the State/Central transmission network/grid. Off-Grid electricity is used through isolated grid and generation is through local renewable source of energy. Here, villagers use the power through local distribution networks.

various Small Hydro Power Projects and has now become a credible catalyst in the Power Sector in the State of Assam.

CASE DESCRIPTION

Mr. Adil and his team met and discussed the idea with the officials of the Government of Assam and agreed to carry out pre-development work for Langsomipi Micro Hydro Scheme in Karbi Anglong District. As a result, State Implementing Agency (Nodal Agency) appointed Assam Power Projects Development Company (APPDCL) to carry out pre-development tasks and also for assistance in implementation of Langsomipi micro hydel scheme.

Accordingly, APPDCL started project development activities for the project in Karbi Anglong district which has many un-electrified villages and hamlets. The stream Langsomipi is a perennial stream and the flow required for the generation of peak load (considering future demand as well) is available even in the leanest season from the proposed micro hydel scheme. The experts from APPDCL visited the villages along with M/s N Arc, hired as a consultant for preparation of Detailed Project Report (DPR)[6] for putting up a micro hydel scheme on the Langsomipi stream with local transmission and distribution network.

The DPR was prepared with completion of following activities by engaging Hydro Experts and Engineers having wide experience in the hydro field. This included:

1. Identification of un-electrified villages near the proposed project.
2. Site Visit, reconnaissance and Topographical Survey studies.
3. Finalisation of suitable Micro Hydel scheme location on the perennial stream.
4. Approval of un-electrified villages from Rural Electrification Wing and Ministry of Non-Renewable Energy Sources.
5. Transmission and distribution studies covering each household/family.
6. Fixation of project capacity based on load requirement of the villages.

A micro hydel scheme of 80 Kilowatt generation capacity was technically feasible at Langsomipi stream in Karbi Anglong District. The Project was envisaged to supply to several un-electrified villages namely Kum Teron, Lambu Teron, Kakati Kro, Long Kathar, Biswanath Pthar, Nihang Rongphar, Kania Terang, and Shirteron with a total of about 160 households of a population of around 900 including power supply to Primary Schools, Dispensary, Flour Mill, Street Light etc. The project generation capacity was planned considering future demand for next five years.

At Langsomipi site, 29 meters head[7] is available for 2 Turbine - Generator units of 40 Kilowatt each. The rate of water flow required will be 0.345 cubic meter per second. This

---

6   DPR – Detailed project report which is prepared after identification of possible site through detailed surveys. It covers basic design aspects of the project, costing and financial aspects besides justification of the project.

7   Head is the difference between water levels at a location where water enters in pipe and location from where water comes out from the Turbine and meets back the river.

flow of water is perennially available in the Langsomipi stream. The Scheme consists of project components like a small concrete diversion weir, a 110 meters long low pressure water pipeline, control valve, water turbine, generator, transformer and transmission/distribution network.

Implementation Process of Langsomipi Micro Hydel Scheme

1. Total project cost for project will be around Rs 60 lakhs.
2. 90% grant is to be received from Central Government after the approval of DPR from Rural Electrification Corporation (REC), Central Public Sector Undertaking (CPSU), and National Hydro Power Corporation (NHPC) in this case.
3. 10% of the funding is to be done by the State Government after approval of DPR.
4. After financial assistance, the contractor will build the project in one year and operate it for the next 5 years.

CURRENT STATUS OF THE LANGSOMIPI MICRO HYDEL SCHEME

After completion of reconnaissance activities, the DPR was submitted by State Nodal Agency to Rural Electrification Corporation (REC). The project was categorised as Decentralised Distributed Generation project (DDG)[8] which are planned for five years keeping future requirements in mind. The first major milestone was achieved successfully. The second step was to get the approval of villages for un-electrified status. This task was also successfully completed and a letter from Village electrification wing of the State and Ministry of Renewable Energy Sources (MNRE) was received conforming that the said villages are still un-electrified. The third step was to get the approval of DPR so that 90% subsidy can be received for implementation of the project. REC forwarded the DPR to review the Hydrology[9] to NHPC. After review of DPR, NHPC advised to install Gauge & Discharge (G&D)[10] measurement sites at the project location to get the daily water flow measurements (Discharge Data) of the stream and to analyse the flow data to generate flow series for carrying out power potential studies. These studies are done for bigger projects and all big rivers in India have G&D sites installed by Central Water Commission for measuring the flow of water on daily basis. Moreover, the State Governments and many private developers have also installed G&D sites at many important rivers/streams

---

[8] Decentralized Distributed Generation (DDG) - Off Gird – The electricity produced is generally fed to the State/Central transmission network/grid. Off-Grid electricity is used through isolated grid and generation is through local renewable source of energy. Here, villagers use the power through local distribution networks.

[9] Rate of flow of water measured and recorded on daily basis (Discharge Data)

[10] G&D – Gauge and Discharge – It measures the flow quantity of water (in cubic meter per second) flowing in the rivers and is recorded on daily basis. The Central Water Commission and State Agencies have installed the G&D sites at all the major rivers in India. However, it is not commercially viable to install the G&D sites at all the small streams in hills.

where big projects are installed or are proposed to be installed. However, the discharge data of very small streams in remote villages is not on record because these are not being measured by any agency and moreover are not considered significant.

As advised by NHPC, G&D Site was installed and discharge data was recorded during the leanest season[11] of the following year to check the minimum flow in the stream. Thereafter, discharge data for the lean season i.e. January till April was also submitted for approval of DPR but after that the instructions came from NHPC to collect the discharge data for 5 years on continuous basis. Consequently State Nodal Agency was not given approval from REC and the project could not make it to the ground and may take some more years. The implementation time of micro hydel scheme is only one year provided all clearances and approval are on table.

As the measurement of discharges for years is not going to serve the purpose, it would have been desirable at NHPC's end if it had approved the DPR for very minimal capacity project as no optimisation studies would have made the difference because capacity was fixed based on the basis of envisaged demand of villagers as well as availability of minimum flow in the stream throughout the year.

As a matter of fact, many such schemes do not come on ground because of rigorous approval processes or lack of focussed approach.

CURRENT CHALLENGES FACED IN IMPLEMENTATION OF MICRO HYDEL SCHEMES

1. In India, micro hydel schemes are evaluated with the same level of detailed studies that are required for small and large hydro projects. Rigorous / optimisation studies for such small schemes are not at all required because these are designed to generate minimum load requirement of the village rather than maximum capacity that can be installed on a particular stream.
2. Too many clearances and delays in obtaining them hamper the implementation of projects which are not commercially oriented but are required for development of society.
3. In consultation with some Indian manufacturers of micro hydel Projects, India should also promote manufacturing facilities for the equipment and standardization of micro hydel turbines. This will help in ensuring off the shelf availability of spare parts at manufacturer's facility including turbine runners and generators, as is the case elsewhere around the world. The non-standardization of project capacities is also causing problem of operation and maintenance of such projects.
4. Most of the micro hydel schemes which are operated by State agencies are not operating well. These are either running at low plant load factor (PLF) [12]or are lying

---

[11]   Leanest season – The Season when the water in the stream/river is minimal amongst all the months/seasons of any year.

[12]   PLF – Plant load factor is ratio of actual power produced to ideal power that is produced from installed project capacity. The approximate PLF band of various sources of energy are Solar projects (19-21%), Wind projects (22-27%), Micro hydel schemes (50- 60%)

abandoned. These micro projects should be operated through local community engagement instead of State Nodal agencies as the latter focus on the small and large projects only. The operation through local community also provides employment, increases skill development and economic development of the area.

RECOMMENDATIONS

1. The Central Government needs to focus on these areas and need to launch district wise campaigns in hilly regions to implement Micro hydel schemes with the involvement of State Government bodies and Community/Panchayats. It is a fact that there is no shortage of funds or technical capabilities in India.
2. Micro hydel schemes are very different from large hydro projects; keeping this in mind, approval from different agencies should be exempted. Even if required, it should be done in a time bound manner.
3. The power demand in remote villages is very low; long-term hydrology studies of perennial stream are not required; hence Gauge & Discharge (G&D) measurement should not be mandatory in such cases.
4. Government of India should take initiative through skill development / Rural employment schemes for promoting micro hydel schemes in hilly regions.

QUESTIONS FOR DISCUSSION

1. What would be the positive impact on environment if micro hydel schemes are implemented in far flung hilly villages?
2. What additional benefits, other than mentioned in case, can be accrued by putting up micro hydel schemes in un-electrified village?
3. What can be done to promote Micro Hydel schemes in village at State and Central level?
4. Compare the pros and cons of various energy sources like Diesel, Solar and Micro Hydro in any un-electrified villages
5. List some of challenges faced by villagers who do not have an access to electricity?

REFERENCES

Boyle, G. & Krishnamurthy, A. (2011). *Taking Charge: Case studies of decentralized renewable energy projects in India in 2010*. Retrieved October 28, 2015, from http://www.greenpeace.org/india/Global/india/report/2011/Taking%20Charge.pdf

ANNEXURE
EXHIBIT 1: ABOUT MICRO HYDEL SCHEME

Micro hydel scheme is a hydro project of less than 100 KW capacity and generation of energy is from potential energy of water. The height of water, known as the "head", is a must for power generation. The head is a natural level difference of two points of river, first point is where water is diverted in Pipe and second point is where water after coming out from turbine meets the river. Two important parameters required for production of hydropower are flow rate of water (Discharge) and a Head. The Micro hydel scheme may be installed with lower head (even > 2 m) and small discharge. In small stream, water discharge may be diverted through pipe known as penstock that can run turbine and generate electricity at desired voltage.

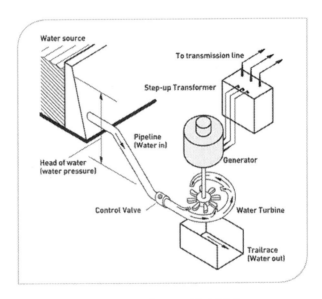

Typical Layout of Micro Hydel Scheme

1. The cost of the project is around INR 0.15 million to INR 0.2 million / KW including transmission, lighting and distribution expense.
2. The plant load factor (PLF) is around 50% to 60%
3. The tariff is around INR 5-6/kWh, but with subsidy from central government which is around 90%, the monthly charges are as low as INR 100 per month per household.

4. Total installation time is 9- 12 months (only after number of approvals and getting financials in place)
5. The comparative cost of diesel through generators generation per unit is more than INR 10/Kwh

BENEFITS OF MICRO HYDEL SCHEMES

1. Electrification of remote villages through round the clock source of energy.
2. Reduction in diesel consumption and reduction of wood cuttings.
3. Employment generation.
4. Irrigation canals can be made and fed through pumping.
5. Useful life of Hydro power projects is 35-50 years. Many micro hydel schemes are running for more than 100 years in India and across the world. However, useful life of Solar and wind projects is 25 years only with lower PLF in comparison with Hydro Projects.

These projects are very easy to install as no Resettlement and Rehabilitation (R&R) issues are involved and implementation time is short, the local public is interested as they will get power there by uplifting their living standards and there are many more reasons to promote projects.

The officials have discussed with Government. of Assam officials and agreed to develop some of the DDG projects in Assam. Finally State Implementing Agency (Nodal Agency) appointed Assam Power Projects Development Company (APPDCL) to carry out pre-development works and for assistance in implementation for two micro hydel schemes.

SECTION

Strategy

CHAPTER 6

Diamond Industry of Surat: Sole Bearer of the Brilliance?

EXECUTIVE SUMMARY

"The beauty of a perfectly cut diamond lies not just in its exquisite aesthetics, but in the way it makes you feel." - Yair Shimansky. Quality of the diamond depends on its source and its cut depends on the experience of the craftsmen. The dominance of India in the global diamond cutting and polishing industry is so high that it accounts for approximately 92% of the world's diamond processing, owing to excellent craftsmanship and cost efficient labor availability. The diamond cutting and polishing industry in Surat, Gujarat has been a significant contributor to Indian economy from a long time, contributing up to 1/6th of the national Gross Domestic Product (GDP). There are a lot of firms in the industry that are working efficiently and producing high quality diamonds.

Some problems have arisen over a period of time and have had a significant impact on the industry's market structure. This case study highlights some problems faced, such as despite the size of the diamond market, the competition is based on non-pricing methods. It was also noted that consumers were loyal to certain firms regardless of the fact that the firms produced only slightly differentiated products and there was a minor difference in prices. Trust can be a big factor in said conditions, monetarily there is always a lot at stake.

Keywords: Diamond Industry, Monopolistic Market, Gray markets, Import Control Laws, Diamond Trading Corporation, De Beers Trading Company (DTC), Surat Diamond Market, Antwerp Diamond Market

NIRAV SAHNI

Nirav is pursuing a Bachelor of Commerce in Finance and Marketing at McGill University in Canada. He has corporate experience from interning at Deloitte in their Financial Advisory Department and has also interned at Sanghavi Diamonds that played an instrumental role in the formation of the case. A keen entrepreneur, Nirav is active in the start-up community currently working on an e-commerce and big data venture: VRentin where he holds the position of the Chief Business Officer. Prior to McGill, Nirav has taken courses in Financial Statistics and Economics at Harvard University where he was ranked amongst the top 5% of his class. An avid learner with interest in Emerging Markets, he has attended conferences at Harvard Business School and Columbia Business School. He has been awarded the Principal's Medal for Excellence in Academics and has also been a state level swimmer in India. He is actively involved in the student community at university and is also a part of the student government. His most recent publication is a case study on the Co-operative Dairy sector in Gujarat that was published by the Case Centre, UK.

Setting the Stage

The president of Surat Diamond Association, Mr. Dineshbhai Navadia and The Gem and Jewellery Export Promotion Council at Surat, Gujarat observed that the diamond market is highly volatile and the businessmen are facing some major challenges in the diamond market owing to fluctuating market parameters. Moreover, many pertinent problems such as emergence of Gray Markets, mismatch between high prices of uncut diamonds and lower polish rates of the diamonds, inconsistent laws and unaccounted market transactions had left the industry in fix.

Organization Background

The Diamond Industry in Surat is so monumental that Surat is renowned as the 'Diamond City' of India. The size of the industry can be gauged by following data. According to the Reserve Bank of India Task Force (2009) there are about 2500 diamond processing units in Surat (RBI Research). Latest estimate by the industry leaders shows that there about 4000 diamond processing units, employing about 400,000 workers excluding indirect employments. There are a small number of large modern factories each employing up to 4000-5000 workers. The medium sized units employ up to 1500-2000 workers and there are a large number of small units employing up to 50 to 100 workers.

The large units are registered units and they are eligible to directly import from mining companies like Rio Tinto, Alrosa and De-Beers. Also, large units sub-contract jobs to small units, which mainly are engaged in cutting, shaping and polishing of diamonds. The medium sized units are primarily engaged in the processing of high quality expensive diamonds. The significance of the Surat Industry could be seen in the fact that 80% of the diamond cutting and polishing of diamonds in India is done in Surat.

In order to understand the structure of the industry, it is mandatory to understand the working of the industry. In the diamond industry there are different players each with different roles and characteristics. The entire process of polishing the raw diamonds constitutes of several tier agents; a few only engaged in imports of raw diamonds whereas the others in processing or exports. The imports are managed through large trading houses such as the Diamond Trading Company (DTC) that aims to sell the diamonds procured from major international suppliers such as the De Beers of South Africa. Other trading houses such as the Hindustan Diamond Company (HDC), Minerals and Metal Trading Corporation of India (MMTC) as well as the National Mineral Development Corporation (NMDC) are involved in importing and selling rough diamonds to potential markets in India such as Mumbai, Surat. These rough diamonds are delivered or sold through small merchants who do not generally have access to the international market as only a few merchants from India approach international markets and initiate the mechanism of sub-contracting raw diamonds to owners of polishing units cum organized home based units.

After the polishing, the value added diamonds follow the same mechanism to reach the trading houses that export the fully processed diamonds in international as well as domestic markets. 95% of the rough diamonds are exported as finished diamonds.

Surat Diamond Industry – The Macro Environment

In the recent past, the diamond industry of Surat is being subjected to fluctuating market parameters due to many pertinent problems and issues.

1. The diamond industry flourished in Surat because skilled labor was available at cheap wages. However, enforcement of minimum wage law is now making the labor expensive, inflating the cost of polishing the uncut diamond.
2. Labor is usually hired on contract basis in order to circumvent Labor Unions and complicated Labor Laws.
3. There is a lot of wastage during polishing to get the diamond in perfect shape according to the desired cut – Princess, Heart, Oval, Marquise, Pear etc. as the diamonds are polished manually.
4. There is a considerable increase in competition due to new entrants in the industry. Entry in the market is easy but sustaining depends on financial backing, as customers are reluctant in making purchases from new players and the other way round as majority of the pruchases and selling is on credit upto 180 days.
5. Indian Banks and Non-Banking Financing Companies (NBFC) are reluctant to offer loans to diamond firms, inspite of charging high rates of interest compared to international banks.
6. Emergence of 'Gray Markets': The data and sales from 'Gray Markets' and unaccounted business could not be recorded but it is causing significant damage to the organized sector.
7. The unaccounted market transactions or the cash transactions in the diamond industry are not taken into consideration while determining the total business. These transactions have the capacity to influence the market. A suggestion was made to remove all taxes (like 1 % central excise duty) and impose a blanket Turnover Tax rate of 2.5% that would make business easier since it would help to know the exact costing of the product for the merchants and also limit the black money transactions.
8. There is a mismatch between high prices of uncut diamonds and lower rates of finished product that is leading to declining demand of the uncut diamond and further widening the demand gap leading to increased acceptance of synthetic diamonds.
9. The menace of lab-cultured diamonds (synthetic diamonds) passing off as natural diamonds in the market is effecting the creditability of Indian diamond industry hence world class Diamond Checking Laboratory with state of the art equipment was established.
10. Many Business houses have set up their offices at Antwerp, Belgium so that the uncut diamond are purchased at competitive price, the Antwerp offices purchase the uncut diamonds and export them to their parent Indian Company which later on after polishing the raw uncut diamond exports them. This is providing them an unfair price advantage over small local players.
11. By setting up offices in Antwerp the large players are also securing loans from International Banks at very marginal interest rates. Further increasing their price advantage.

12. The Diamond Industries are installing latest state of art computerized diamond cutting & polishing machines, in order have minimum waste and have exquisite finish in order to compete against Bangkok and Russia who offers better polished diamonds at cost effective prices.

13. Formation of state laws such as import control laws or protectionist measures like tariffs or quotas etc. can influence the market as well. Also, laws against collusion change pricing strategies amongst producers.

14. Diamantaires are unable to get supply of rough diamonds worth $12 billion through SNZ (Special Notified Zone) at Mumbai because specific guidelines on taxation have still not been set by the Ministry of Finance.

15. The credit cycle plays an important role in the high value transactions and is highly affected by the volatile dollar exchange rates. The National Mineral Development Corporation (NMDC) is should consider playing an active role in minimizing the impact of the fluctuating dollar on the industry.

16. Lack of relevant courses at prestigious institutions like IIT's and IIM's has resulted in scarcity of skilled human capital for value added services compared to markets such as Hong Kong, Bangkok, Japan, China, America where such courses and training are available and is contributing to significant profits for the industry.

MARKET ANALYSIS

To resolve the problems and come up with appropriate solutions, studies were carried out using Varacha, Surat as a sample and on the basis of interviews with various officials from the Surat Diamond Association, leading diamond merchants and consumers, the following observations were made:

SIZE OF THE DIAMOND INDUSTRY

The size of the diamond industry is measured in terms of the sellers of diamonds. It is estimated that there are at least 1100 merchants and a large number of diamond cutting units also operating from their houses. The high number of firms is reported due to the potential investment returns seen in the industry. Moreover, the availability of skilled labor including technically competent diamond cutters is a prime factor for the large market size as well. Hence, the diamond trading houses in 'Varacha' is mostly looked as a family business by most due to the small-scale nature of the industry.

BARRIERS TO ENTRY/EXIT

Upon interview with Mr. Dineshbhai Navadia, President of the Surat Diamond Association, it was noted that the barriers to entry and exit do not exist to a high extent in the market. Any number of sellers can enter the market subject to condition they have the adequate capacity, capital and labor. The sellers can leave the market without any impact on the market as there are a large number of firms and a few firms don't have an impact on the whole market. It was also noted in the interview that it is a rare case where a single producer is able to influence the price of the product. Another fact noted was that the new sellers joining the market might find it challenging to sell the processed diamonds due to the competition being faced by other dominant sellers in the market.

After studying the conditions of established diamond markets i.e. Belgium and Dubai, it was observed that the barriers faced by Indian merchants could be completely overcome if the economic policies in India regarding diamond trading were replaced by policies that are used by Belgium and Dubai.

HOMOGENOUS PRODUCTS

An initial look at the diamonds processed in the 'Varacha' industry might seem to be similar or identical. The data accrued from interviews indicated that the diamonds might be similar from the external structure as they are from the same carbon isotope but differ in terms of minute characteristics such as quality, purity, color and shape.

The diamond 'Round' seems similar from the external structure however it is different in terms of internal structure. So, it is treated as two different products. This is mainly because this affects the value of the diamond measure in terms of carats. It was observed that the diamonds are mainly differentiated based on the '3 C's', which are Carat, Clarity and Cut. So, the rough diamonds that comes in as homogenous products are slightly differentiated once processed. However, there are also cases where the type of diamond being sold is different and is not very common in the market. This leads to the firm making supernormal profits in the short run.

PERFECT KNOWLEDGE

'Knowledge' refers to the awareness and information related to the market and its dynamic aspects such as supply-demand and prices. Perfect knowledge means that both producers and suppliers are aware of all necessary information such as price, cost of production, sales etc. However, it was noted from the consumer survey that the consumers do not contact many sellers before buying the product and 87% of the consumers were unaware of the details of the price and the product in the market.

Hence, the degree of imperfect knowledge is highlighted in the industry that mainly arises due to promotional schemes like zero interest, credit and flat percent discount schemes etc. These instruments are used to divert the consumers from reaching other sellers and remain loyal to the specific sellers for reasons such as honesty, transparency and reasonable price margins. Also about 44% of the consumers only visit one seller before buying diamonds, so they are not aware of others.

PRICE AGREEMENTS BETWEEN FIRMS

The Diamond Industry of Surat at times tends to agree on certain prices at which they will sell the product in the market. This collusion creates an artificial supply constraint leading to supernormal profits. If the firms were to only make normal profits and not operate in a collusive oligopoly the diamond would be sold at the same price as the cost where only the opportunity cost is covered.

COMPETITION IN THE MARKET

The extent and nature of competitiveness in the diamond market is based on two folds; the quality of the diamonds and the characteristics of the collusion that occurs. This makes it evident that the firms do not compete on price as the price is sometime fixed for a short period of time in the market. It was also noted that non-price factors attract the consumers. However, collusion is just an exception and a unique case that does not last for long, as there are a lot of firms in the market. It would also be ineffective as for 95 % of the consumers, the demand is elastic.

However, the price wars do exist but at a very initial stage and to the extent of bottom margins, promoting sale. The non-price factor includes 'consumer loyalty' and 'trust,' the diamond industry has huge transactions made every day and the purchase is not made that often. 89% of the consumers buy from the same seller whereas only 11% change sellers.

There are only special occasions or events that lead to a large sale of diamonds so a decrease in the price does not always result in an increase in the demand. It could also foreshadow that the product is not of the desired quality and could damage the reputation of the merchant as well. Thus, the level of competition in the market is high but not only subjected to the price.

PROFITABILITY

The profit margins are a key factor as well in determining the structure of the market. They are a function of resource and cost, highlighting a margin in the industry. This could be seen in the following table:

Table 1: Profits for 'Varacha' markets

	Amount (Million $)
Imports of Rough Diamonds	4559
Exports of Finished Diamonds	6775
Value Added	2406

Source: (Annual Report GJEPC)

Thus, margins on an average could be within the range of 17-22%, which is very high for an industry operating on such a large scale and having such a large number of firms. The supernormal profits could be even higher due to the collusion of a few large companies leading to the formation of an oligopoly. Soon, this is shifted back to normal profits due to the new entrants in the market.

CONCLUSION

The research findings can be summarized as-

1. According to the consumer survey and the data interpreted from it, it could be inferred that the consumers have a high degree of loyalty towards certain firms, as the product is of high value and mutual trust between buyer and seller is key.
2. The analysis from the survey and the data brings about the fact that a fall in the prices does not always lead to an increase in the demand for the product. This may be because the consumers are brand loyal and they are indifferent to prices in the market.
3. Due to the price agreements between firms that lead to the formation of collusion along with the non-price competition strategies; the structure resembles an oligopoly.

QUESTIONS FOR DISCUSSION

1. Discuss the impact of Consumer Loyalty on sale of high value goods.
2. State and elaborate two other goods, where fall in prices does not necessarily mean an increase in demand.
3. State the reasons for Surat being an inseparable part of the World Diamond Processing industry.
4. Discuss the market structure of Surat Diamond Processing Industry.

REFERENCES

Stonier, A.W., and Hague, D.C. (1973). *A Textbook of Economic Theory*. New York: Wiley.

Thomas, M.R. (2013, 16 December). *Small diamond units struggle to get new tech*. Retrieved October 15, 2015, from http://timesofindia.indiatimes.com/city/surat/Small-diamond-units-struggle-to-get-new-tech/articleshow/27453677.cms

CHAPTER 7

Money Times - At the Crossroads

EXECUTIVE SUMMARY

The National Sales Head of 'Money Times' Ram Mehta is facing an uphill task of stagnating revenues in the last few years. The financial paper was an addition to the MS Media group's portfolio of leading English & Hindi brands.

While operating in a challenged macro ecosystem, the management pundits are of the firm opinion that players who can think big, leverage multiple monetization models and invest in content shall have a competitive advantage. The brand marketing team had conducted a survey in the six major metro cities among the senior corporate/self-employed professionals (Mostly male) in the age group 25-44 years. The recommendations of market research highlighted existing need gaps and paved the way of brand differentiation related to product size, design and content. Rather than launching another "Me Too" product, the management was clear since the very inception to break existing paradigms in Business paper journalism.

The brand was launched with a cutting edge design, high end analytical content and had a clear second positioning from the beginning in terms of circulation and readership. The emphasis on Personal Finance opened up a new segment of corporate women readers along with the already existing male readers, increasing its scope and appeal. It is believed, professionals wanted to be seen reading and talking about the product resulting in a certain snob value. The differentiated product was giving a very positive rub off to the group's portfolio.

However the excitement was short-lived as the management failed to address certain business issues. Institutional sales and product visibility were limited and had scope for immense improvement as per market feedback. The perception of the product was in extremes - It found immense support among the CXO community but had limited liking at the lower and the middle management levels. Rigid edit policies were not finding much favor with the statutory advertisers who preferred flexibility in rates and placements.

Ram Mehta has been working on a bucket list to enhance revenue monetization. Post analysis of MIS data, market feedback, sales reviews etc., Ram proposes series of initiatives for revenue growth.

Keywords: Brand Differentiation, Business Paper, Turnaround Strategy, Sales Growth, Advertising, Strategy.

GAUTAM SRIVASTAVA

Gautam is Physics (Hons) from Fergusson College, Pune and MBA from The Institute of Management, Development & Research, Pune. He started his career in Sales from Modi Xerox where he learnt the nuances of sales process, honing his skills in the bargain. Selling photocopiers to his major account The Times of India marked his entry to the media industry. Apart from sales he got an in-depth exposure to Operations, Customer Service & Execution. He has performed key roles in Media TransAsia, Diligent Media Corporation & HT Media Ltd in a career spanning two and a half decades and handling various portfolios, involving leadership roles related to revenue management and leading large teams. He has had a rich exposure to start ups by setting up of the Delhi branch of DNA newspaper. He has also been the internal lead for Soft Skills training utilizing the SPANCO process which was initiated by Xerox and followed by every major Sales player globally.

He currently drives the statutory business nationally at HT Media Ltd. in Delhi

CHALLENGED MACRO ENVIRONMENT

Leadership team of MS Media summons Ram Mehta, National Sales Head of Money Times (MT). MT was launched in April 2009 to create a niche in the financial newspaper market and had achieved a clear second position in the business paper space in circulation and readership. However national advertising revenue had been static in the last few years in spite of achieving the above milestone.

Table 1: Circulation Figures

Year	2010	2011	2012	2013	2014
Revenue(INR Billion)	20.5	21.9	20.8	21.1	19.5

Ram Mehta was clearly at the crossroads. Muted GDP growth, high interest rates, poor domestic demand and deficient rainfall had affected consumer sentiments. Advertising budgets were under pressure. Volumes in business papers were stressed and were dominated by advertisements of industry bodies, few corporate campaigns, business to business event led communications, statutory financial advertisements, tender and statutory notices, few international campaigns etc. resulting in low revenue realization.

ORGANIZATION BACKGROUND

M.S. Media Group was founded in the post-independence era of India with the launch of their first English daily - The India Times. The promoter S.P Mishra had philanthropic considerations rather than pure commercial interest for the newspaper and wanted the product to play its part as the watchdog of the society and be known for objectivity as well as honest journalism. Gradual expansion led to a circulation of over 1.4 million. In February 1987 their Hindi daily, Hindi Times was launched from the Hindi heartland city of Bhopal. Robust expansion of their Hindi edition was fuelled by the growing rural economy, high aspiration levels of the Indian middle class especially in the mini metros, increasing awareness and growth in income levels. The group currently has 15 Hindi editions with a circulation of over 1.6 million copies. The group closed last financial year with a turnover over of INR 240 Billion with advertising and circulation revenues being in the ratio of 85:15.

The company is being managed and run by a team of highly motivated professionals who have had distinguished careers and come from diverse backgrounds including Fast Moving Consumer Goods Industry, Banking Services, Organized Retail etc. Immense importance is given to competence during hiring as it strongly feels that people are its greatest asset. It has nearly 3000 employees on board with a robust management structure with a core think tank team to provide vision and strategic direction to take the company to the next level of growth. The company runs an aggressive rewards and recognition program and believes in highlighting excellence to foster a sense of pride in its employees. It has an open organizational culture and encourages ideation for broader perspectives. It has a strong MIS team in place for sales support, trend analysis, and potential opportunity area monetization and fosters a robust analytical approach to problem solving. The digitization process has already gained momentum with innovation being encouraged at every step so that it could become a more reliable and consistent player. The sales team utilizes the CRM module for meeting the twin objectives of customer acquisition and retention. Special emphasis is given to train its employees as the organization strongly feels that honing the skills of its employees is fundamental to growth and being relevant in the highly competitive and dynamic media space.

SETTING THE STAGE

Money Times was conceived with the basic premise of addressing the existing gaps in financial journalism and to deliver a cutting edge product to its customers. Global experts were involved during the launch of Money Times to surpass current standards in design and content which was not seen before from the perspective of a business daily. Money Times was the result from an organization which leveraged technology to the hilt with differentiated content being its core philosophy in order to gain competitive advantage. It had a global appeal, crisp editorial articles, excellent reproduction quality and analytical perspective. It also had various leading brands' advertisements across verticals.

CASE DESCRIPTION - MARKET RESEARCH FINDINGS & STRATEGY

Nearly all existing financial brands were pink in colour, broadsheet and largely catered to the financial business community. Content was filled with heavy financial jargon, dominated by corporate finance and had little coverage on personal finance. The CEO of the MS Media group did not want to launch another "Me Too" product which would blur brand differentiation and dilute their value proposition. Three areas were identified for brand differentiation - product size and design, content and ease of product navigation.

The world's most renowned newspaper designer Robert Cain was hired to bring in the design and size element differentiation. Dimensions of the final product were kept 24 cms. width and 44 cms. height. The new size facilitated navigation with relative ease and kept in the mind the morning metro commuters to work.

For content a partnership was struck with the world's leading financial paper group of Europe - The International Tribune, which was considered to be the flag bearer of Financial Journalism globally. It had been instrumental in changing many governments in its 63 years of existence. It had nearly half a million paid subscribers for its web edition with an annual subscription fee of 49 euros.

The essence of content strategy was to simplify financial journalism to widen its appeal and also cater to the working women segment in the age group of 30-45 years. They wanted to jargonize business news. Trends were reflecting the changing preferences of the upwardly mobile readers so that they could gain more value from the differentiated content. Personal Finance was the biggest focus area as the readers preferred news which they could use. This was a challenge as well as an opportunity area for the newspaper groups as widening the scope of their content meant potential new readers which would further augment their product's readership base.

STAFFING STRATEGY

To give the product a distinct flavour no existing journalist was transferred from the group company to MT. Global exposure, technical proficiency, domain expertise, analytical approach etc. were some of the critical factors which formed the basis of recruitment. More than 60% of the newly recruited staff had global exposure and many had worked with leading international groups. With the exception of the Business Head being from within the group, the National Sales Head, accounts team and their first line staff were a mix from the media and other sectors. All key verticals like Automobile, Durable, Fast Moving Consumer Goods, Financial Services were allotted to stand alone teams.

LAUNCH & MARKET STANDING

In April 2009 the Delhi and Mumbai editions of Money Times (MT) were launched marking the group's entry in the financial segment with a circulation of 40000 copies. Delhi and Mumbai represent the two biggest markets for the print advertising industry. The management was willing to leverage the existing sales strength to work out large revenue commitment deals from prospective advertisers. MT was the undisputed second lead in the financial paper market in the country from its inception. MT currently has 10 editions with a circulation of 275000 copies and a readership of 475000 as per audited newspaper agency reports.

CHALLENGES FACING THE ORGANIZATION - THE VERDICT

Readers accepted Money Times as a brilliant product signifying a paradigm shift in the product size and design element. Some of its uniqueness lay in extremely high quality content, news analysis, in depth journalism, quality reproduction and unbiased objectivity. There was great emphasis on personal finance and on news which offered immense value to the discerning readers. The product delivered a high readership appeal among the working women in the age group 30-45 years. There were weekly columns on health, wellness, technology, media, finance, insurance etc. giving fresh insights and analysis to the readers. Their editorial coverage resulted in improved goodwill among the advertising fraternity and helped garner incremental business. The reader and advertiser response to the product was mixed. The senior management levels had a high level of acceptance. Readers in the middle management levels were neutral and executives down the line preferred and advertised with the other financial dailies who were flexible with advertising rates and positioning of their advertisements as they felt that the editorial policy of MT related to the commercial interests of the advertising department was very rigid.

ACTION PLAN AND THE WAY FORWARD

1. Some of the possibilities for Ram Mehta to improve his stagnating revenues are:
2. Initial Public Offer (IPO) Monetization-Focus on the Small and Medium Enterprise segment clients with issue size ranging from INR 1-5 Billion.
3. Clients filing Draft Red Herring Prospectus with Securities and Exchange Board of India on the increase with improving investment climate. Tap such clients proactively by constantly scanning websites of Bombay Stock Exchange and Money Control.

4. Increase financial share of advertising with the private clients.
5. Execute State Government features nationally.
6. Professional MOU's - tie up with industry bodies like Confederation of Indian Industry (CII), The Federation of Indian Chambers of Commerce and Industry (FICCI), The Associated Chambers of Commerce and Industry of India (ASSOCHAM).
7. Events monetization - Organize quarterly high profile events under the Money Times branding with adequate sponsorship revenue.
8. Build events platform around Disruptive Technology and Innovation, HR Excellence, Financial Inclusion, Role of Private Universities, Regulatory hurdles in the real estate space etc.
9. Tap Financial Results/Statutory notice advertisements of Public Sector Units (PSU)/ Banks, nationally as they enjoy high rate realization.
10. Key Accounts Management - Build relationships with key personnel in the various organisations by inviting them to the Money Times events and networking with them.
11. Ensure adequate editorial coverage of the financial results and analysis of the top 250 companies listed on the Bombay Stock Exchange.
12. Explore the idea of starting a Company Secretaries round table event in Money Times - Build regular connect with them through the MT newsletter and regular emailers.
13. Tap existing database of clients who organise events around niche domains ranging from single to 4-5 main events within the country. They normally prefer business papers as a medium of choice to showcase their events for sponsorships and delegate participation.
14. Enhanced focus on government tender notifications for higher revenue monetisation.
15. Explore the possibility of initiatives centred on Corporate Social Responsibility with the major public sector advertisers.
16. Open up inorganic revenue streams by focussing on segments like International Exhibitions.

QUESTIONS FOR DISCUSSION

1. Was the launch of Money Times ahead of its time?
2. Did the brand marketing team do justice to the product in terms of its positioning, Institutional Sales, visibility and reach?
3. Are business papers stretched for revenues and readership in the era of digitalisation?
4. Is the company leveraging its equity enough to ensure adequate monetisation of the financial product?
5. Is the size of the product a limitation in the process of garnering revenues?

SECTION

International Business

CHAPTER 8

Dealing With Culture – Striving For Success in a Flourishing Market

EXECUTIVE SUMMARY

Since 2005, two wheeler industry in India has exhibited constant change. There are three defining factors for this - influx of foreign competition, heightened competition among domestic players, and increasing customer expectations. As a part of this industry Excel Motors, a family owned two wheeler company, had to take two major business decisions. The first decision was about the strategy for business expansion, and the second was its renewed focus on scooters. It considered various factors before expansion into a foreign market. The case assesses the need to conduct consumer research prior to expansion of operations into a new market; the factors involved in choosing the right form of research to conduct; and subsequently finding the right partner to execute it. It also discusses how insights gained by the consumer research are subsequently used effectively by Excel Motors to take actionable business decisions.

Keywords: Consumer Research, International Market, Marketing Channels, Market Development, Market Research, Qualitative Research, Scooters, Two-Wheeler Market

HAVISH MADHVAPATY

Havish works as Head – Research with Traverse Strategy Consultants, a research and consulting start up. An MBA Gold Medallist, he started his career with Reckitt Benckiser, post which he worked as a research scholar, and subsequently as an Assistant Professor. During his stint in academics, his academic research work has been published extensively in national and international journals, and he presented his work at leading institutions across the country such as IMT Ghaziabad, IMI New Delhi, IIT Roorkee, JNU etc.

He is a certified Microsoft Office Specialist (MOS) Excel 2013 and VSkills certified Digital Marketing Master.

Presently he leads a team of analysts at Traverse, and spearheads all research work. He has created models for Brand Ranking, CMO Ranking and Experiential Marketing. He has worked on projects for clients from various sectors around the world, including various ministries of Government of India.

SETTING THE STAGE

Ayush Singh was feeling exhilarated. He had just given a 2 hour presentation to Parag Bisht - National Sales Head, Excel Motors and Prabir Rao, National Marketing Head, Excel Motors. The international operations that he heads had performed well and he had surpassed his targets. The company had now renewed its focus on scooters – a category that they first exited, and then re-entered noticing the changing market trends. Ayush presented a snapshot of Bangladesh market to Parag and Prabir, with focus on the potential of launching scooters in Bangladesh followed by Nepal and Sri Lanka. The meeting went reasonably well and Ayush got the opportunity to present his business strategy, although he realized that things would be much tougher than he originally anticipated.

CASE DESCRIPTION

Ayush Singh has been with Excel Motors for 7 years. He joined the company as a Management Trainee and grew up the ranks to become a Zonal Manager. Two years ago Excel Motors first began their international expansion into Bangladesh, Nepal, and Sri Lanka. Ayush had been promoted as Manager, International Operations to look after these regions. He had been delighted for being selected for the profile, considering there were many other equally qualified candidates. He had initially refused the movement since he would be required to travel 15 days every month and would not be able to spend time with his family. Eventually he did agree to the posting since it was a matter of pride to be chosen by the company for such an important assignment. For the last two years, he had successfully guided Excel Motors' international expansion. While motorcycles had done well, Excel Motors wanted to now focus on scooters in the international markets. Ayush was therefore asked to prepare a presentation to be shown to his reporting managers.

ORGANIZATION BACKGROUND

Excel Motors is a family owned company that was founded in Mumbai, India in 1971 by Mr. Raman Katyal. Excel Motors enjoyed massive success as the only scooter manufacturer in the country for 2 decades. In the 1990s consumer preferences shifted towards motorcycles and Excel motors haplessly watched as new players were attracting customers - who were now shifting to motorcycles. Post the liberalization of Indian economy in early 1990's a lot of foreign players had also entered the Indian two wheeler market. Reacting to the competition Excel Motors started to focus on the motorcycle business and launched motorcycles. On the basis of the positive response received for their motorcycles and the constantly weakening sales for scooters, they eventually decided to exit the scooter business in 2000. Unfortunately for Excel Motors, the decision turned out to be untimely. After the company exited the scooter market in 2000, there had been a steady increase in scooter ridership, with the last few years showing accelerated growth. Every two-wheeler company was now targeting the scooter market again. Excel Motors also now decided to refocus on the scooter market.

Last few years reaped success for Excel Motors, and in India their scooter sales grew at a much faster pace than their motorcycle sales. Realizing that there is immense opportunity for growth in international markets, Excel Motors went on an expansion drive with plans to develop international operations focusing specifically on scooters.

Table 1: Average annual sales in units for two wheeler industry

				(all figures in '000)
Period	1996-2000	2001-2005	2006-2010	2011-2015
Average Annual Total Two Wheeler Sales	202	222	235	240
Average Annual Motorcycle Sales	175	170	165	120
Average Annual Scooter Sales	27	52	70	120

BUSINESS CHALLENGE

The objective of the meeting for Ayush was to meet Parag and Prabir and discuss opportunities for launching two new scooters named Alpha and Amazer in the international markets. Both scooters had been successfully selling in India for a year now. There were a few other Indian players in the three international markets selling scooters, but it was only a half-hearted pitch. Percentage of scooters to the overall two wheeler sales in the three regions was below 1%.

Parag felt there was a huge potential in the market and since the market was untapped for scooters they would have a first mover advantage. Prabir though – while sharing the belief that the market will grow one day – was more cautious, and did not share the same level of enthusiasm. Prabir felt that marketing spend should happen only after the market is more developed.

During this discussion, Ayush was asked for his opinion on the scooter market. Ayush was very cautious with his use of words since he knew that if he gives a commitment on sale figures, the company would expect him to deliver. He was also a little worried about the rift between Parag and Prabir since both had contrasting viewpoints. While Parag felt that there should be high marketing spends to increase scooter sales, Prabir was not committed to spend money on marketing unless the market first showed potential. Since Ayush reported directly to both the marketing and sales heads, he knew that picking sides would not be a wise decision. He therefore decided to take out some time and think about it. He requested Parag and Prabir to allow him a few days to come up with a plan.

The challenge faced by Ayush was manifold – marketing and sales of scooters, launch of a new product category; while also dealing with differing opinions of his reporting managers.

CHOOSING THE RIGHT APPROACH - MARKET RESEARCH

Ayush considered various options, and decided that it would be unwise to jump right into the market, and decided to get market research done. He presented this thought to Parag and Prabir who then told him that they could only sanction a budget of INR 500,000. Ayush was completely taken aback since he knew that with such limited funds it would be very difficult to get research done on a large scale. There were several factors that he had to take into account:

1. Primary research vs. secondary research
2. Large full-service research firm vs. boutique firm
3. Type of survey methodologies
4. Respondent sample size and break up
5. Locations for conducting research

Ayush gave all these factors a lot of thought and considered the pros and cons of each alternative. He eventually decided on three key points:

1. Get research done only in Bangladesh.
2. Do qualitative research.
3. Hire a boutique research firm.

He chose Bangladesh as the test market since he felt the country had a lot of cultural similarities to India. He also decided to get qualitative research done since he did not merely want to fill up an excel file with details of respondents. He felt he must probe consumer sentiments and try to understand in detail their psyche when deciding to purchase a two wheeler.

He also decided to hire Yureka Research, a two year old start-up specializing in qualitative research based out of India. He did not choose the large, established research agencies since he knew from prior experience that the larger firms would ultimately outsource work to some small local research firm. Also, for qualitative research the larger research agency would complete the task but not bother to analyse deeply the customer purchase factors, their motivations, and their hindrances. The larger research agency would be rigid and not accept suggestions, and would not offer him the flexibility of making improvisations to the research midway.

Ayush therefore got in touch with Yureka Research, and they came up with a plan to get the research conducted over a 6 day period. Yureka was charging INR 475,000 for the research project. He was also very satisfied with the research plan presented by them. Yureka would hire a local team for Bangladesh. This was integral since in qualitative research having a local team would allow better connection with the respondents. This in turn would lead to more detailed and articulated responses.

The next big question was to choose the geographical scope and the research methodologies. Dhaka and Dinajpur were chosen as the two locations for the research. Dhaka being a metropolitan city would be a market most open to usage of scooters.

Dinajpur as a rural town was representative of the demographics of about 90% of Bangladesh.

There were 200 respondents chosen for the research. They decided to choose a combination of owners and non-owners, and intenders (intending to purchase a two-wheeler in the next one year) vs. non-intenders.

Table 2: Respondent break up

Respondent Type	Non Intenders	Intenders
Current Owners – Two Wheelers	42	77
Non Owners – Two Wheelers	33	48

They chose a two stage research process – where the first stage was a Group Discussion, followed by Central Location Testing[1] (CLT) where a questionnaire would be administered. (*See Exhibit 1*) The research process was:

1. Group Discussion with respondents.

    There were 8 – 12 respondents in a group, along with the moderator. At this point the respondents were not told that the research was being conducted for Excel Motors. They were asked to discuss the scooter market in general. Each group discussion lasted 45 minutes to an hour.

    The following points were used as catalysts for discussion:

    a.   Do you / someone in your family own a two wheeler?
    b.   How many brands did you consider prior to purchasing?
    c.   When did you purchase a two wheeler?
    d.   How long did the process take?
    e.   What was the process of your last purchase?
    f.   How many people influenced your purchase?
    g.   How satisfied / dissatisfied were you with purchase? Why?
    h.   What is the proportion of scooters compared to motorcycles in market?
    i.   What do you think of when scooters are mentioned as a category?
    j.   What is general perception of scooters? They are intended for which customers?
    k.   What are advantages and disadvantages of scooters over motorcycles?
    l.   Do you think people know about these?
    m.   What do you think is the awareness level of scooters in the market?
    n.   Are companies doing enough advertising of scooters?
    o.   Are companies doing enough brand awareness activities for scooters?
    p.   If yes, what activities? Are these activities successful/unsuccessful? Why?

---

[1]   Central location tests are a type of Quantitative research technique. They are product marketing tests performed in controlled environments, contrary to home-user tests, which take place where the products would actually be used.

2. Product Demonstration.

   Post the group discussion the respondents were given a product demo of the two scooters. The scooters were labelled with stickers – masking the fact that they belonged to Excel Motors.

3. Static feedback

   First phase of questionnaire was administered based on static feedback of the two scooters. Here the respondents were shown the scooters and were asked to rate different features based on their visual observation of the scooter.

4. Test Ride

   The respondents chose one of the two scooters and took a test ride.

5. Dynamic feedback

   Second phase of questionnaire was administered based on dynamic feedback of the scooter based on the test ride taken by customers. This was conducted post the test ride and respondents were asked to rate different parameters based on the test ride.

   Ayush was himself a part of few group discussions as an observer. This gave him insights into the consumer mind-set.

   Ayush also ensured that there were females in a few groups to see if there was a change in the responses. In Dhaka - having a more liberal society apropos female ridership of scooters - one group was assigned as an all-female group with 8 female respondents. This allowed him to gauge and compare responses of both males and females. Most importantly, since Bangladesh was a predominantly Muslim and a male dominated country, he felt that if there are only females in a group, they would be able to express their true feelings more clearly.

   These were the observations and key insights that came from the Group Discussion:

1. Scooters are generally associated with women – but both Male / Female respondents were open to both Male / Female riding it.

   This was a very interesting insight to Ayush since prior to the research he had thought that there would be very strong inhibitions surrounding female ridership. As it turned out this was not the case.

2. In terms of perception, respondents felt scooters offer better manoeuvrability but less power when compared to motorcycles.

3. Respondents said that they had never had the chance to ride a scooter since no one they knew, owned one. Also scooters were rarely available at dealers.

4. The respondents said that the target market for scooters is from the age group 18 – 25 years and then 40+ years.

5. Respondents said that one clear advantage of scooters is that everyone in the family can ride it.

6. Youngsters chose social media as the advertising medium of their choice. Television commercials and billboards were chosen by all respondent types.

7. Scooters advertisements only feature Indian brand ambassadors and are telecast on Indian channels. Respondents said they would prefer to see Bangladeshi actors / cricketers as the brand ambassadors and on Bangladeshi channels.

8. Respondents said Dhaka should be a test market for scooters since other parts of Bangladesh would look at Dhaka and take inspiration to try the same products.

These were the key observations from the test ride:

1. Control and leg space was highly appreciated.
2. Manoeuvrability was rated well – despite the fact that a gearless two wheeler was new to the respondents.
3. Low sound was also appreciated.
4. There was an increase in how respondents rated scooters versus motorcycles pre–ride and post–ride.

Table 3: Respondent satisfaction pre ride and post ride

	Control	Acceleration	Seating comfort	Turning ease	Braking
Pre Ride	60.00%	34.00%	48.00%	48.00%	38.00%
Post Ride	72.00%	45.00%	68.00%	68.00%	60.00%

5. Lack of footbrake came as a surprise.
6. Suggested price of scooters was given at 15% - 20% lower than motorcycles of similar cubic capacity (cc).

RECOMMENDATIONS

Ayush - armed with all the insights went to Parag and Prabir, and they were happy with the various points that came out. It was clear that inhibitions and culture do not play as big a part as everyone originally anticipated. It was also evident that marketing had to ensure that people are encouraged to take test rides of the scooters. Ayush therefore had the approval from Excel Motors to launch scooters in the country. Ayush realized that now he had to devise his strategy to launch scooters in the Bangladesh market successfully. He therefore looked at the Ansoff Matrix.

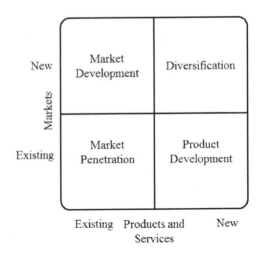

Figure 1: Ansoff Matrix

Ayush studied all of them in detail; trying to identify the correct strategy / combination of strategies:

1. Market penetration, in the lower left quadrant, was the safest of the four options. Here, the focus was on expanding sales of existing product in existing market, since it is known the product works and that the market holds few surprises.
   - Ayush did not consider this step since scooters were a new product category.
2. Product development, in the lower right quadrant, was slightly more risky, because here a new product was introduced into an existing market.
   - This was a very important aspect for Ayush, since a new product was being launched into the market where he had already managed to create a brand presence of motorcycles. There was an element of risk here because if scooters failed to sell in the market, the negative sentiment would also affect motorcycles.
3. Market development, in the upper left quadrant, put an existing product into an entirely new market. This was done by finding a new use for the product, or by adding new features or benefits to it.
   - Ayush considered some takeaways from this quadrant as well, as he would be taking the successful scooters selling in India and do some customization to suit customer tastes in Bangladesh.
4. Diversification, in the upper right quadrant, was the riskiest of the four options, because here a new, unproven product was being introduced into an entirely new market which might not be fully understood.
   - Ayush was not considering this step since Bangladesh was not an entirely new market for them.

Ayush now had to decide the steps he needs to take to launch scooters in the Bangladesh market. He had decided to first focus on market development using social media, influencer marketing campaigns, road shows etc. Dhaka would be the first market where the marketing shall be done and slowly marketing shall be expanded to other parts of the country.

QUESTIONS FOR DISCUSSION

1. Did Ayush choose the right research agency and the right research technique for the type of research considering his objective?
2. Are the insights generated from the research sufficient for the task at hand? What type of future research would you recommend?
3. What should be the stages of market entry opted by Ayush? Who should he choose as the target group?
4. How should scooters be positioned? What marketing mediums should be used for advertising and promotion?
5. What are the overall motivation factors and hindrances when it comes to selling scooters in Bangladesh?

APPENDIX

Exhibit 1: EXCEL MOTORS SCOOTER SURVEY (Questionnaire)

EXCEL MOTORS SCOOTER SURVEY

INTRODUCTION

Hello Sir, we are conducting a research to understand scooter market and consumer behaviour in Bangladesh. You have been selected for this survey, which will be around 15 - 20 minutes long, followed by a test ride.

Name: _____
Address: _____
Phone No: _____
Occupation: _____

AWARENESS AND PAST PURCHASE

1.1 Do you own a two wheeler?

Yes
No

(If No, skip to 1.8)

1.2 Which brand of two-wheeler do you presently own?

_____

1.3 How long have you owned it?

_____

1.4 Who were the influencers of this purchase? (Mention in order of importance)

_____

1.5 Why do you use a two wheeler? (Mention in order of importance)

_____

1.6 What are the things you like / dislike about owning a motorcycle?

Like	Dislike

1.7 Rate the following on the basis of your own experience with your purchase. (1 – Bad, 5 – Excellent)

Price	
Mileage	
Features	
Handling in traffic	
Turning ease	
Ride comfort	
Multifamily usage	
Maintenance	
Attractiveness	

1.8 What are the words that come top of your mind when I say "Scooters"?

_____

1.9 Are you considering purchase of a two wheeler in next 6 months?

Yes
No

(If Yes, ask 1.9.1; If No, jump to 1.9.2)

1.9.1
Which brands are you considering, and why?

Brand	**Reason**

(Now go to 1.10)

1.9.2 If you do consider a purchase in future, which brands will you consider, and why?

Brand	Reason

1.10 Which brands of two wheelers can you recall, and which ones do you think makes scooters?

Brand	Scooters (Y/N)	Brand Name of Scooters

1.11 1.11 Can you recall ads of any scooters? Can you recall the ad?

Brand	Type of ad	Remark

STATIC EVALUATION

2.1 What are the first few things that you like about the scooter (in order of importance)? Why?

(First List, then ask why?)

Alpha

Amazer

2.2 What are the first few things that you dislike about the scooter (in order of importance)? Why?

(First List, then ask why?)

Alpha

Amazer

2.3 What are the special features that you see in the scooter?

Alpha	Amazer

2.4 Rate the importance of the following features to you? (1 – Not Important at all, 5 – Very Important)

Alpha		Amazer	
Gearless		Gearless	
Mobile charging port		Mobile charging port	
Helmet compartment		Helmet compartment	
Integrated braking		Integrated braking	
Plastic body		Metallic body	
Aggressive graphics		Single tone colour with emblem	
Immobilizer			
Tubeless Tyres		Tubeless Tyres	
Body Style – Front		Body Style – Front	
Body Style – Rear		Body Style – Rear	
Body Style – Side		Body Style – Side	
Height		Height	
Instrument Cluster		Instrument Cluster	
Front Storage Area		Front Storage Area	
Exhaust		Exhaust	

2.5 Which colours would you prefer?

Alpha	Amazer

2.6 After looking at these features, at what price would you like to buy this?

Alpha   _____

Amazer   _____

2.7 Which one of these scooters would you prefer?

Alpha

Amazer

2.8 In comparison to a motorcycle, rate the following which you expect in the ride:

	Scooter better	At par	Motorcycle better
Control			
Acceleration			
Seating comfort			
Turning ease			
Braking			

DYNAMIC EVALUATION

3.1 What are your thoughts on the ride?

3.2 How would you rate the ride overall (1 – Bad, 5 – Excellent)?

_____

3.3 Name three things about the ride that you did not expect?

_____

_____

_____

3.4 Now that you have taken a ride, in comparison to a motorcycle, rate the following:

	Scooter better	At par	Motorcycle better
Control			
Acceleration			
Seating comfort			
Turning ease			
Braking			

3.5 What would be the three things you would like to change in the scooter, based on the ride?

_____

3.6 What would be the three things you would like to recommend to someone, based on the ride?

_____

3.7 Who would you choose as the ideal brand ambassador for these scooters, and why?

3.8 After looking at ride quality, at what price would you like to buy this? (Figures in Bangladesh Taka)

120000 – 130000
130001 – 140000
140001 – 150000
150000 – 160000

3.9 Who do you think will like this product?

(Ask about Age, Family members, Income level, Usage etc.)

THANK YOU

CHAPTER 9

Pisces Group: Maiden Voyage

EXECUTIVE SUMMARY:

With the focus of people shifting towards nutrition and their efforts to improve their diets; the Frozen Seafood business, a part of FMCG industry is a lucrative investment opportunity. The rising demand for frozen food items is owing to the increasingly busy schedule of people. Frozen food is a welcome convenience to them, people buy in large quantities and store for later use. It helps the institutional buyers like restaurants, hotels and caterers as well; buying in bulk quantities gives them a price advantage.

Unlike the rural areas where fresh meats and fish are readily available the story is not the same in urban areas, where the quality of the products is questionable especially in fast perishable items such as fish. The local water bodies are mostly polluted in cities and towns even as the rivers are fed with industrial waste, and the general practice is that the fishermen go fishing in the morning and sell the catch in the evening, compromising on the freshness of the catch.

Freezing the fish increases the shelf life of the fish, it is easy to store and convenient to use later on. Having caught on this trend early and banking on the growth of the market; Mr. Amit Shah, Chairman of Pisces Group had taken his company to unscaled heights. He was now a renowned name in the Fast Moving Consumer Goods (FMCG) Industry, whom others viewed as a serious competitor. Mr. Shah understood a developing company like his could increase its business by expanding its product line, or expanding the geographical reach of its products – making them available to new customers.

The geographical expansion can be local or international depending upon the capability and aspirations of the organization. There can be multiple ways to enter a new market – Exporting, Licensing, Joint Venture and Direct Investment. This case aims to analyse the possibilities of entering the Central African market for an International FMCG Company starting with Rwanda. The focus for Mr. Shah will be on direct investment in the form of a wholly owned subsidiary; which can be in the form of Greenfield Investment or Acquisition depending upon the market analysis.

It is of utmost importance for a successful investment to understand the culture of the host country. Culture plays a deterministic role in the food habits of the people, which is very significant for a FMCG company before making entry in a market. Pisces Group Chairman Mr. Amit Shah is now seeking answers for the investment questions.

Keywords: Global Business Development, India - Rwanda, Africa, Fisheries, Fast Moving Consumer Goods (FMCG)

PRATEEK MANGAL

Prateek works as the Director – Client Services for SSR Management Consultants Pvt. Ltd. An MBA from Indian Institute of Foreign Trade, Kolkata and International University in Geneva, Switzerland, he started his corporate journey with Triton Management Services and served the FMCG giant in Africa and India. He is widely travelled and experienced across Europe, Africa and Asia and has six year of experience in FMCG and Manufacturing Industry.

He has a passion to gather knowledge and is also a Diploma holder in Cyber Law from Asian School of Cyber Laws, Pune. He has also been part of numerous Conclaves and Symposiums and has presented and published research papers on key FMCG and Manufacturing issues.

SETTING THE STAGE

Mr. Amit Shah is sitting in deep thought, gazing out, watching the sunset in the ocean from the window of his 11th floor office at Nariman Point, Mumbai. He has called upon an emergency meeting of top management in an hour. The report from the Rwanda team has just come in. It's time to take a decision – Is it the right place? Is it the right time?

In 1995, India was also waking up to a wave of Industrialization after the Industrial reforms policy of 1991; Mr. Shah had realized the growth potential of an emerging market and set up the India operations of Pisces Group. The group has since then employed industry experts, professionals, MBA graduates with diverse background to further drive the growth of Pisces Group.

Pisces group was growing steadily for 12 years by strategically expanding geographical boundaries as well as introducing newer business verticals with investments pouring in from Asia and USA. In 2007, the company was 900 strong and was generating a profit of USD $320 million. Suddenly the world was facing the economic downturn of 2007-2008, it was a global crisis and the markets were on the brink of collapse. Pisces Group also lost a lot of business; they had to close shops in many countries in West Africa they had recently commenced operations in. Indian distribution business also took a major hit. Profits dried up, the company was fighting to manage distribution with the increase in raw material prices from all the major suppliers. Mr. Shah was fighting hard to absorb the blow from the falling sales. The year 2007 also saw the outbreak of Avian Influenza (Bird Flu) in poultry produce in Western Africa, poultry sales took a nosedive, poultry farms were closed and the produce destroyed. The future looked bleak but an eternal optimist and a valiant man, Mr. Shah weathered the raging storm with the support of hardworking workforce of the company. After 3 years; they had taken major hits, surviving on the sales of seafood's majorly as the sales of poultry and meats had dried up after the outbreak of Avian Influenza, lot of business was lost but it was time to regroup and restart.

6 MONTHS EARLIER

To regain the lost geography and expand rapidly Mr. Shah decided to infuse some new blood in the company, he selected a handful of talented individuals from top B-Schools of India and trained them in business tactics in India and Africa to handle and develop the business. The young appointees were given the rank of Management Trainees (MT's) and were trained in Business Development – Identifying an opportunity, developing market entry strategy, developing partnership in the host nation. They were also given inputs for location handing aspects of currently existing markets – sales and planning, operations and inventory, finances and engineering (cold storages).

It was now time for action; Mr. Shah summoned Pranav Mathur and Tej Pratap, two talented recruits from the management trainee team and gave them the responsibility of collecting the relevant data from Rwanda.

Ecstatic with the opportunity the two young management trainees were determined to make the best of it. They had a busy time ahead of them, there was a complete business development trip to plan and execute. They were given a budget of USD 4000 and 15 days to collect the required information. The first things for Pranav and Tej were to book accommodation for them and get the travel desk at company's corporate office to book return flights to Rwanda on specified dates. Along with planning the itinerary they had to apply for Visa of Rwanda. The duo was in Delhi in no time to apply for a Visa at the Rwandan High Commission at Vasant Vihar, New Delhi. They weighed in all Visa options, Corporate Visa was not a possibility as they did not have any business contact in the host country to extend an invitation for a corporate visit so they decided to apply for a Single-Entry Tourist Visa and get the work done. After some documentation and verification they got the Visa for travel.

Back in Mumbai, they started planning their trip with information gathering. Their basic tasks as outlined by the management were collecting information about dairy, meat and other proteins and their consumption patterns. Their administrative task was collecting information about setting up and running a business concern, along with entry regulations and restrictions for a multinational venturing in Rwanda. They also had to identify concerned stakeholders such as Carrier and Forwarder (C&F), Wholesalers, Importers etc. and forging business ties with them. They had to find logistic and storage partners and get a quote on the cost of transportation and storage from them. They had to extensively study the actual geographical terrain, demographics, language and cultural beliefs. They had to gauge possible interest of shopkeepers for the company's products by conducting market visits and observing the buying pattern of populace for different food items. Apart from this they also had to compile all this information, analyse it and provide their input in the report suggesting if Rwanda was an ideal place for investment.

They started with gathering contacts and addresses of related Government Offices, Lawyers, Chartered Accountants and Logistics service providers or Transporters over the internet. It was followed by sending emails intimating of their visit and purpose to fix appointments with them. Language did not pose a barrier as English was one of the languages other than French and Kinyarwanda; Swahili was prevalent in the rural areas as per the information available online. One commendable feature they noted was that Rwanda had set up "Rwanda Development Board (RDB)" – which was a one stop solution for all the information, permits and clearance for setting up and operating a business in the country. All the government departments were brought under one roof, at the RDB Office.

Time flew during the preparations and it was time for Pranav and Tej to leave for Rwanda. They were to leave from Terminal 3 of IGI Airport at New Delhi; after checking in and passing through the emigration channel they were waiting for their flight to be announced when the enormity of all this started to sink in to them, they were thinking and planning – how to minimize the stay, lower the expenses and gather maximum information at the same time. They had a critical decision for such a big company in their hands, the responsibility was paramount and they did not want to let Mr. Shah down. Their Ethiopian Air flight was a pleasant one, with a hop at 'Adis Ababa' they landed at 'Kigali' the capital of Rwanda. The airport was albeit a small one and they had to walk to the terminal building. To their delight English was spoken more than they had anticipated and the airport staff was cooperative.

After passing through the immigration channel, collecting their baggage and exiting the terminal they took a Taxi from the Kigali Airport. With the horses of their imagination galloping, they found their first avenue to save some money, they asked the taxi driver to take them to a cost efficient hotel and not the one they had pre-booked.

Normally, it is not a safe thing to do in Africa but their research showed Rwanda, unlike other African countries was a safe destination. It is the only country in Africa that has zero percent corruption and minimal crime rate. After reaching the hotel they decided to freshen up and head straight away to the RDB office without wasting a moment, time was not their friend in this exercise.

Over the course of the week; they met RDB Officials for understanding the entry and operating requirements for a multinational organization. They met 'Minagri' Officials i.e. the officials from Rwandan Ministry of Agriculture; who provided the data of cattle, poultry, dairy and fisheries production and consumption in the country. They also met several lawyers to understand their terms and conditions as well as the role they will be playing from the setting up of a new company all the way to settling of any professional disputes that the company may face later on. They met Chartered Accountants to understand the tax filing and profit sharing structure in the country and they also met several Transporters to assess and select a logistic partner if and when necessary, recording quotes for operations from all of them. The meetings with Lawyers, Chartered Accountants and Transporters were an information gathering and relationship building exercise. All this while, they had found an Indian restaurant and made it their hangout, post the working hours, made friends with the owner and patrons from India and neighbouring countries, seeking help with information collection.

The subsequent week, the young managers had marked their itinerary for market visits and geographical and demographical surveys; the statistical data for the same were available from RDB but it was time to assess the ground realities. Culturally, the people of Rwanda are not much of meat eaters, the cattle they owned mainly served as a status symbol and a symbol of wealth. Pranav and Tej, riding pillion on motorbike taxis went far and wide to local villages, wholesale and retail markets as well as to different super-markets and marts in the city area. They also found details of couple of butcher houses in the outskirts of Kigali and visited them to assess any business opportunities. The run so far had been dismal to say the least in terms of business prospects; the opportunities were not looking exceptional from the trip but the boys struck gold at the butcher houses. The butcher houses had recently got export clearances and were exporting beef all over Africa.

The fifteen day long trip was nearing its end. Pranav and Tej had succeeded in their task of data collection and observation of the ground realities. They had made some friends and developed some relationships which they had to foster and turn into a long term business association as per the decisions made by the management after submission of the compiled report.

ORGANIZATIONAL BACKGROUND

Pisces group started as Pisces Management Company Pvt. Ltd. in the year 1995 with an interest in commodity trading and distribution. It had a humble start in Mumbai, Maharashtra, India; with plans to make it big in the Food and Nutrition business. Today it is a 20 year old conglomerate comprising of about 35 different companies, employing more than 1500 people engaged in farming, trading and processing of poultry, meat and seafood in Asia, Africa, Europe and the Middle East with an annual turnover of over USD 700 million.

Pisces Group was founded by its chairman Mr. Amit Shah, an alumnus of Harvard Business School. Mr. Shah started his career as a charted accountant for an FMCG company in Abuja, Nigeria in early 1980's with his hard work and dedication he quickly rose through the ranks and reached the post of General Manager (Accounts) in less than 6 years. Thereafter he left the company and joined a Seafood Trading Company as General Manager and left the company 8 years later as Business Head of Frozen Seafood Division. Understanding the tremendous growth potential of the fisheries business and the African market and having gotten a hold on the nuances of the business Mr. Shah decided to become an entrepreneur and founded the FMCG giant that is Pisces Group today. With his expertise and dedication the business expanded quickly to West African countries such as Nigeria, Ghana, Togo, Benin, and Côte d'Ivoire. The products were made to suit local tastes and the packaging was eye catching. Sales were picking up and Pisces Group soon became the market leader in poultry, seafood; trading and distribution. The business model of having wholly owned subsidiaries was a success, a few Indians in decision making capacities leading the local work force and working in tandem with local authorities, were running the locations smoothly.

ORGANIZATIONAL CHALLENGES

To run a location in a foreign country, Pisces group typically posted 3-4 Indians in management positions and 12-20 local staff for various other tasks, the local staff would increase in number depending upon the business at the location. The Indians were paid INR 1.5-2.0 million per year in Indian currency and a local allowance of USD 150-400. The local staff was paid USD 100-200 per month. To be a profitable location, at least sell 5000 Tons of fish should be sold every month.

Selling fisheries is a push process; products have to be sold by educating the customers. Most customers are not aware of is that the "Fresh" sea fish that they buy from the market is normally 10-14 days old and only iced for preservation. Fishermen head out to the sea on small trawlers, they sail for about a couple of days to reach the fishing location. They fish for 2-3 days depending on the catch size. By the time they reach back to the docks with their catch, the first days catch in already 5 days old. From the docs the fish is then iced, boxed and sent to interior locations though roadways, which take another 5-7 days. The fish are sold for another 2-4 days at the destination market. As a fast perishing item fishes are in terrible state by the time they reach the consumers.

In the alternate scenario, the catch at the docks is purchased by the agents of the seafood processing companies. The fish are then transported to a nearby facility where they are cleaned, gutted, cured and Individually Quick Frozen (IQF) or Batch Frozen in blast freezers and then packed, palletized and stored in cold storages or transported to destination in Reefer (refrigerated) containers.

Normally, a 20 feet reefer container has a payload capacity of 15-18 tons of fish and 12-15 tons of cephalopods (crustaceans). A 40 feet container has payload capacity of up to 30 tons. The cost of a fish like- Mackerel ranges from $700-$1300 per ton, and are sold in the market for $4- $8 per kg. Sardines cost $800-$1200 per ton and are sold $14-$18 per kg; another favourite Tilapia costs $700-$1100 per ton with the selling price of $5-$8 per kg. Business orders are a minimum of a container (28 tons) for purchase in each case.

An educated customer always makes the smart choice but due to lack of information and at times in order to save some money, people prefer purchasing the raw, iced fish rather than the cured, frozen and packed version. This makes it hard for the organized retail or FMCG companies to sell their products in the open market and get loyal customers for their products. Hence, for Pisces group emphasis is on organizational sale of the products to hotels, restaurants and eateries but it involves additional costs as well. Organizational buyers are always a tough nut to crack and allow little margin for profit for the sellers.

CURRENT CHALLENGES

Back in Mumbai after their eventful trip of fifteen days Pranav and Tej sat in the corporate office and analysed all the data. Based on their observation they were of the opinion that Rwanda was not a place to invest but it would definitely be profitable to source beef from there, for export to Middle East countries. Exporting to Europe flashed in their minds too but they decided against mentioning it in the report as the import restrictions are much more stringent in European countries.

The young MT's then carefully compiled their report making it a point to cover all the points from the visit and submitted it to the 'Strategy Team', who would study the report and further submit it to the management. The duo now sat in anticipation... what will be the call of the management on this? Will Rwanda see them again?

QUESTIONS FOR DISCUSSION

1. Do you concur with the recommendation in the report?
2. What are your views on the report, considering yourself to be Mr. Amit Shah, would you invest in Rwanda?
3. As a Senior Level Manager in the company do you feel the need to expand as Pisces Management Company?
4. Based on the information provided, what do you think of Rwanda as an Investment Destination?

REFERENCES

Adekunle, J. (2007). *Culture and Customs of Rwanda*. Connecticut: Greenwood Publishing Group.

Rwanda Demographics Profile 2014. (n.d.). Retrieved December 10, 2015, from http://www.indexmundi.com/rwanda/demographics_profile.html

Strategic & Investment Plan To Strengthen Meat Industry In Rwanda. (2012, July). Retrieved December 15, 2015, from http://www.minagri.gov.rw/fileadmin/user_upload/documents/STRAT.PLC/Final_report_Rwanda_Meat_industry_final.pdf

APPENDIX

1. Country Report: Rwanda

COUNTRY PROFILE

Rwanda, officially the Republic of Rwanda, is a sovereign state in central and east Africa. It is in the Great Lakes region of Africa and is highly elevated; its geography dominated by mountains in the western and savanna to the eastern side, with numerous lakes present throughout the country. The population is young and predominantly rural, with a density among the highest in Africa.

Geography

At 26,338 square kilometres, Rwanda is the world's 149th-largest country. The entire country is at a high altitude: the lowest point is the Rusizi River at 950 meters above sea level. Rwanda is bordered by the DRC (Democratic Republic of the Congo) to the west, Tanzania to the east, Uganda to the north, and Burundi to the south. It lies a few degrees south of the equator and is landlocked. The capital, Kigali, is located near the centre of Rwanda and is the only major city and economic centre.

Economy

The country has GDP of USD 7.890 billion and per-capita GNI of USD 700 and is a low income economy. Major exported items are Coffee, spices and Ores; the major markets include China, Germany, and the United States. The economy is managed by the central National Bank of Rwanda and the currency is the Rwandan franc; the exchange rate floats from 740-755 francs to the United States dollar.

Demographics

As of 2015, the National Institute of Statistics of Rwanda estimated Rwanda's population to be 11,262,564. The 2012 census had recorded a population of 10,515,973. The population is young: in the 2012 census, 43.3% of the population was aged 15 and under, and 53.4% were between 16 and 64. The annual birth rate is estimated at 40.2 births per 1,000 inhabitants in 2015, and the death rate at 14.9. At 445 inhabitants per square kilometre, Rwanda's population density is amongst the highest in Africa.

MAJOR CITIES

Kigali, with population of more than 1 million (2012), is the capital and largest city of Rwanda. It is situated near the geographic center of the nation and is the only urbanized city. The city has been the economic, cultural, and transport hub of Rwanda since it became capital at independence in 1962.

GROUND LEVEL REPORT

In Rwanda, the country has less than 20 percent population living in urban areas, mainly centered in and around the capital city Kigali. The per capita GNI is USD 700 with approximately 45 percent of the population living below poverty line. The local populace is paid meagre salaries of 10,000RF to 25,000RF for a month's labor; most members of the family are employed in menial jobs.

Animals here serve primarily as symbols of wealth and status for the people rather than as a source of protein. Most people consume meat only about twice a month, people living near lakes ate fish, in particular Tilapia. The per capita meat consumption in Rwanda (below10 kg/year) is very low as compared to African average (32 kg/year). People have low inclination for meat consumption; the reason could be low purchasing power of the people.

Rwanda's largest fresh water lake, Lake Kivu is very poor in fish fauna; totalling to 28 species including introduced species and is prone to "Limnic eruptions" (lake overturns) due to volcanic activity.

Portek East Africa Terminals Limited handles Rwanda's main inland cargo handling facility located near the capital city of Kigali. The dry port handles almost 90% of the goods imported to, transiting through and exported from Rwanda. Nearest shipping ports Mombasa and Dar e Salaam are more than 1400 Kilometres away. The Rwandan government is in the process of planning a connecting railway from Rwanda to the Tanzanian port of Dar e Salaam. Road transport is the main form of goods transportation. There are over 14,000 kilometers of roadways in the country of which the majority is unpaved. Rwanda does not have a rail transportation system, but uses the railroad systems of neighbouring countries like Tanzania, Uganda and Kenya as transit routes for goods originating from or destined for Rwanda.

Cattle populations in Rwanda are given in the table below, it should be noted the growth rate of cattle has lowered in the recent years due to the lack of available land for rearing of cattle.

Livestock	2011	2012	2013(est.)	2014(est.)	2015(Act.)
Cattle	1 143 553	1 135 141	1 132 810	1 132 810	1 335 000
Sheep	630 860	635 860	649 860	656 860	799 000
Goat	2 532 277	2 732 277	3 032 277	3 432 277	2 971 000
Pigs	716 629	806 629	906 629	1 016 629	706 000
Rabbits	828 802	978 802	1 128 802	1 303 802	844 700
Poultry	3 890 274	4 790 274	5 790 274	6 890 274	4 081 000

Source: Strategic & Investment Plan to Strengthen Meat
Industry in Rwanda, 2012 www.minagri.rw

Market Survey

Major Supermarkets

1. UTC Nakumatt (located in Union Trade Center), has: Butcher, Bakery, Produce, Frozen goods, Refrigerated goods, Imported products.
2. KCT Nakumatt (located in Kigali City Tower), has: Butcher, Bakery, Produce, Frozen goods, Refrigerated goods, Imported products.
3. Simba Supermarket; has: Butcher, Bakery, Produce, Dried Goods, Cafe and some frozen and refrigerated goods.

Local Protein Prices

Commodity	Avg. Price	Price Range	Avg. Price (In USD)
Eggs (12)	1,248.00 RF	1,200.00-1,440.00	$1.68
Local Cheese (1kg)	4,124.34 RF	2,500.00-7,000.00	$5.54
Chicken Breasts (Boneless, Skinless), (1kg)	4,247.58 RF	3,200.00-6,000.00	$5.71
Beef Round (1kg) (or Equivalent Back Leg Red Meat)	2,750.00 RF	2,500.00-3,000.00	$3.70
Fish (Tilapia), (1 kg)	1,350.00 RF	1,200.00-1,500.00	$1.81
Water (1.5 liter bottle)	871.43 RF	600.00-1,200.00	$1.17

Source: www.numbeo.com, www.newtimes.co.rw

Utilities/Rent (Monthly)

	Avg. Cost	Range	Avg. Cost (In USD)
Apartment (3 bedrooms) in City Centre	430,000.00 RF	300,000.00-600,000.00 RF	$5,780
Commercial Space (500 sq. ft.)		5,000,000-9,000,000 RF	$5,700 – $12,100
Cold Storage (200 tons)	Not Available		
Basic (Electricity, Heating, Water, Garbage) for 85m2 Apartment	36,000.00 RF	30,000.00-45,000.00 RF	$48.39

1 min. of Prepaid Mobile Tariff Local (No Discounts or Plans)	57.50 RF	55.00-60.00 RF	$0.08
Internet (10 Mbps, Unlimited Data, Cable/ADSL)	212,000.00 RF	20,000.00-280,000.00 RF	$284.95
Gasoline (1 liter)	909.33 RF	810.00-1,000.00 RF	$1.22

Source: www.numbeo.com

RECOMMENDATIONS

At ground level fisheries does not offer much to begin with in Rwanda, coupled with the fact that there is an additional cost of transportation to the tune of USD 5000 per container (Reefer Containers) to bring it from the port cities Mombasa (Kenya) or Dar-e-Salaam (Tanzania), to Kigali. This additional cost takes out a huge chunk from our margin per container. Additionally, there is a shortage of cold storage space; we need to build a cold storage to start a business.

Only opportunity in Rwanda can be of sourcing beef for trading or export purposes; as the country has recently received a regional export license after nationwide inspection by experts from the World Animal Health Organization.

* *This report is for educational purposes only.*

SECTION

Finance

CHAPTER 10

ISCE Crisis: The Deficit of Trust

EXECUTIVE SUMMARY

The Indian Spot Commodity Exchange (ISCE) incorporated in 2008 by Trading Softwares India Ltd. (TSIL) came under scrutiny in April 2013 after it violated the provisions set by the Forward Markets Commission (FMC). ISCE is an electronic, institutionalized national level spot exchange. It provides a platform to farmers for selling their produce and to traders, exporters and investors for buying this produce on an electronic trading platform. This spot exchange is an online trading platform based on the delivery of standard contracts which have specific delivery time. Contrary to the normal operations in the exchange, Mr. Aditya Rathore, an investigating officer of FMC found that ISCE allowed trading even without verifying the physical stocks. It demonstrated that ISCE allowed "short sales" by its members on the trading platform. Mr. Rathore also found out that ISCE violated the provisions set by Forward Contracts Regulation Act, 1952[1]. The contracts with settlement period of more than 11 days which were not transferable and were specific delivery contracts traded on the exchange. It resulted in a massive problem in the year 2013, as the amount for payouts had accumulated to approximately INR 72 Billion.

Lack of knowledge and lack of information related to the underlying instruments on the investor's part led to such kind of scam. The ISCE scam has again highlighted the fear over investment opportunities and investment safety. Ponzi schemes have always made the investors question the safety of different investment avenues. It is questionable therefore why ISCE regulators didn't notice that trading had been happening in pair trades with more than "T+11" settlement period since 2008 and why investors invested in financial instruments, even when they are not aware of structural details and trading arrangements of the instruments.

Keywords: Spot Exchange, Commodity Trading, Warehouse Receipt, Investment Scam, Ponzi Scheme, Investor's Awareness.

DIKSHITA

Dikshita, M.Sc. (Mathematics), MIFA, CFA (ICFAI), is an option analyst for Index options and has experience in banking and in trading of stocks based on technical analysis. She has participated and presented papers in National Conference and Seminar.

---

[1] Under the Forward Contracts Regulation Act 1952, the spot contract has a maximum period of settlement for 11 days i.e. the transfer of money and delivery of goods must happen within "T+11" days.

Dr. Harjit Singh

Dr. Singh, B.Ed., MFC (Gold Medalist), MBA, M.Phil., PhD, is an Associate Professor in Amity School of Business, Amity University, Noida. He has vast teaching experience at Postgraduate and Corporate level. He is a regular contributor to National and International journals and has participated and presented papers in several National and International Seminars. He has authored two text books and has written several study material books for reputed universities and institutes. Besides this, he has numerous case studies, research papers, chapters, book reviews to his credit. He is the editor of some reputed journals and an Academic Counsellor at IGNOU.

SETTING THE STAGE

It was April 2015; Mr. Aditya Rathore was feeling the sweat form on his face even in the chill of his air-conditioned office and thinking about the recently exposed ISCE (Indian Spot Commodity Exchange) scam in his jurisdiction involving huge sums of money to the tune of INR 72 Billion. Coming out of his chain of thoughts, he switched on the television and saw the news of the ISCE Scam flashing on all news channels and making headlines. Investors were protesting outside Kerala High court in Ernakulam for their lost money, whereas the High Court refused to intervene in ISCE scam involving DN Proteins and several other renowned names. Sinking back into his thoughts, Mr. Rathore, the investigating officer from Forward Market Commission (FMC) started theorizing that because of no early intervention by the Government, the scam had already cost the investors billions of their hard earned money.

In August 2014, the Economic Offences Wing (EOW) of Bengaluru Police had already arrested default borrowers: Dhruvan Naik (DN Proteins), Chandresh Naidu (Rose Refineries), Samath Vaidyan (SV Agroprocessors), Nageshwaran Reddy (Reddy Foods), Karthik Nair (K.N. Imports), Thangaraj Pai (T.P. Sugar), Bhavyesh Prabhu (Prabhu Projects), Ilaiyaraja Nair (I.N. Agrotech), Mallesh Kurup (Kurup & Sons Agrotech), Nagarajan Thampi (Cotton Yarn Textiles), Trinath Shetty (Metal Alloys & Industries) (Exhibit 1).

The investigation reports filed by Mr. Rathore to FMC suggested that the founder of ISCE, Mr. Chiranjeev Iyer had approved all the fraudulent contracts. As a result, fresh charge sheet was filed by FMC against Mr. Chiranjeev Iyer and his trusted member of ISCE, Mr. Ekachakra Pandit. Mumbai police interrogated both of them and they were charged as the masterminds behind the ISCE Scam.

Arrests had been made, but still no solution was reported to trace and recover investors' money. The only possible solution which Mr. Rathore could see was the merger of Trading Softwares India Ltd (TSIL) and Indian Spot Commodity Exchange (ISCE) in order to give back the investors' money because their money already had been lavished away by the default borrowers. While thinking about the possible solutions in order to recover the investors' money, Mr. Rathore went back to the time when he had sent the notice on behalf of FMC to ISCE for the first time. They were asked to stop conducting trade because of mismatch in their record books. It was notable how non-intervention by the Department of Consumer Affairs (DCA) had led this scam to reach INR 72 Billion. "Why ISCE was given exemptions from the strict regulations which were mandatory to be followed by any commodity exchange" led Mr. Rathore to go for further investigations.

ORGANIZATIONAL BACKGROUND

Chiranjeev Iyer had started his career as an engineer for the Bombay Stock Exchange (BSE) on the BSE's Online Trading System (BOLT) system in 1990. After learning the nuances of the business, Iyer formed a company named Trading Softwares India Ltd (TSIL) in 1996 and started establishing TSIL as a big name in providing back-office support for brokerage firms and terminal software for trading in India. He then formed Indian Multi Commodity Exchange Limited (IMCEL) and few other exchanges in India as well as abroad.

The Indian Spot Commodity Exchange (ISCE) was promoted as a spot exchange for commodities by Trading Softwares India Ltd. (TSIL) and National Commodities Marketing Federation of India Limited (NCFED). NCFED was given 100 shares as a token by ISCE so that the brand name NCFED could be used and ISCE could be hyped as "farmer's market[2]". It was an institutionalized national level spot exchange which provided an electronic trading platform. It provided solutions for the problems seen by the exporters, processors, importers, traders, farmers and the investors. ISCE commenced live trading operations for the first time in different commodities on 15th October 2008. It had started with trading in pre-certified cotton bales for delivery in Bengaluru and imported gold and silver bars for delivery in Ernakulam, and after that, a number of commodities were added to the existing portfolio. ISCE gave a platform to farmers for selling their produce. Traders, exporters, and investors bought this produce on the electronic trading platform. This spot exchange was an online trading platform based on the delivery of standard contracts with a specific delivery time. ISCE was established to help the farmers to access the trading market through an exchange and in return get good prices for their produce.

Iyer used his influence to get exemptions for ISCE in regard to "short sales", "verification of stocks" and "settlement within T+11 days" from the Department of Consumer Affairs.

Services offered by ISCE:

1. Selling - It provided an electronic trading platform as well as an auction platform to sell commodities (Bullion, Agro-products, and Metals).
2. Procurement - Bulk buyers used to acquire or buy the agro-commodities from the farmers directly on the electronic trading platform.
3. Warehousing - It provided warehouses at different locations for different commodities and also helped in selling the commodities on the electronic trading platform to purchasers or millers situated at different locations across the country.
4. Investment – It also launched investment instruments like E-series products which can be bought by the investors and kept in the Demat account, the way shares in the equity market are bought and kept. E-Copper, E-Silver, and E-Gold were available to the investors.
5. Arbitrage - A trader had an arbitrage opportunity by trading at different prices available for the same commodity.

Facilities offered by ISCE:

1. Trading with a delivery obligation on a daily basis as well on a net basis.
2. Demat facility was available for delivery of the commodity.
3. If any trading contract remained unsettled at the end of the day then it would get automatically settled by compulsory delivery.

---

[2]   A farmers' market is a normal market where farmers and producers sell produce from their fields. They sell the commodities directly to the consumers or buyers in farmers' market.

4. Interchangeability of the same commodity between Indian Spot Commodity Exchange (ISCE) and Indian Multi-Commodity Exchange Limited (IMCEL) because of common International Commodities Identification Number (ICIN) numbers.
5. Loan facility was available against pledge of demat / warehouse receipt.
6. Arbitrage opportunity in cash/futures (a derivative of the commodity).

CASE DESCRIPTION

Commodity markets are in the emerging phase as compared to the stock market in context to demand and supply scenario. The growth of Indian Spot commodity Exchange (ISCE) had been significant in comparison to the growth of different commodity exchanges from America, Europe, and Asia. As an investing avenue, ISCE platform was used for trading, arbitraging, speculation etc. in different commodities in India.

EXECUTION OF TRADE IN ISCE

Forward Market Commission (FMC) regulates the rules and regulations that govern commodity trading. Under the Forward Contracts Regulation Act 1952, the spot contract has a maximum period of settlement for 11 days i.e. the transfer of money and delivery of goods must happen within "T+11" days. The contracts with "T+11" settlement period were trading in Indian Spot Commodity Exchange (ISCE).

In ISCE, trading was being conducted by buying and selling a commodity. Seller and buyer would make a contract on an agreed upon price for a pre-specified date. ISCE being an electronic trading platform gave benefit to the buyers and sellers of contract that they can be at different locations and still buy and sell their commodities in the form of contracts. ISCE gave a guarantee to the buyers and sellers of the contract that exchange would ensure the settlement of the contract. In case of default by the buyer, that means if he does not pay the money, be it any reason; the exchange would sell the commodity to some other buyer and settle the contract. Similarly, if the seller defaults, the exchange would settle the contract. To make sure everything is well conducted, ISCE made sure that the seller would come to a warehouse designated by exchange and submit his goods for testing and verification of quality and weight. In return, he would get a "warehouse receipt" that he uses for trading on the electronic platform provided. This warehouse receipt when traded, would entitle the buyer to get the commodities from the warehouse. Apart from this, the buyer could keep goods in the warehouse also by paying the rental charges for the warehouse.

WHAT WENT WRONG?

ISCE was conceived for improved price realization to farmers, bringing transparency in price and arbitrage opportunities for the trading community as well for investors. ISCE was incorporated with the purpose to be in sync with already existing commodity markets and to give synergy in the existing process of markets. It had brought three entities together – the contract buyers, the sellers of the commodities and the investors. Investors were the ones who were actually funding the transactions. Investors received interest amount as a profit on the transaction which they had financed. The buyers paid a premium (some differential amount) in order to settle the contracts. The final payout actually gave the benefits to the financiers or investors.

Contrary to the normal operations in the exchange, Mr. Rathore as the investigating officer from FMC found that ISCE allowed trading without even verifying the stocks which in turn showed that they had allowed short sales by the members on their trading platform. He also found out that ISCE violated the provisions set by Forward Contract Regulation Act 1952, as the contracts with settlement period of more than 11 days which were not transferable and were specific delivery contracts were traded on the exchange. The problem spiralled out of control when amount linked in the unsettled payouts came to be INR 72 Billion as on July 29, 2013. As a result of this, trading got suspended in ISCE and the launch of new contracts was also suspended. As if this was not enough, Mr. Rathore observed that ISCE had also violated the demutualization rule, as it was an entity owned by the Trading Softwares India Ltd headed by Chiranjeev Iyer.

Further, it turned out to be a scam which looped in the sellers, investors, and borrowers. In the investigations, it was found that the forward contracts were used by the speculators and investors so as to make money. In the forward contracts section, few commodity stockists were involved in selling the warehouse receipts to investors so as to get payments upfront. The investors involved in this also sold the commodities to the stockists after 25 to 35 days to make sure the buyback arrangement happened and in all this, they ignored the regulations set up by FMC. Trading in forwards contracts with this kind of buyback arrangement led the stockists to receive money upfront and investors got their returns. It was also found that this led to earning of 12%-14% returns for the investors.

In his investigation, Mr. Rathore noticed that investors traded the contracts without the proof of the underlying commodity being present in the warehouse. The investors had established buyback arrangements after selling commodities at ISCE without verifying the availability of underlying commodity. Inventories maintained were fictitious, certain commodities like sugar and metals as well as other commodities were not in sync with record books as shown in the Exhibit 2.

Investors were not aware of structural details and trading arrangements of the instruments in which they had invested. Lack of information and knowledge related to underlying instruments raised the amount of unsettled pay-outs to INR 72 Billion as on July 29th, 2013. The ISCE scam had again raised concerns over investment opportunities and their safety.

THE PONZI SCHEME[3]

There was a financing problem which was highlighted when it was reported that the contracts were being traded in pairs. To get a clear glimpse of the trading situation in ISCE, consider an example: If a plant owner processing a certain commodity could not get a loan sanctioned from the bank; he would borrow the money from the investors at 15-18

---

[3]   A Ponzi scheme is a fictitious investment project or scheme where an individual or an organization, gives returns to its investors from new funds paid to the organization by new investors, rather than from profit earned by the organization.

percent interest. That interest percentage would be noticeably less than the percentage that banks charged. Then knowing that the goods which he would be selling to somebody would remain at the warehouse; the next step would be cheating the customer by assuring him that he would add some more quantity to the warehouse. Over the telephonic conversation, he would convince the customer to agree to his proposal. So in this way, he created increased quantity of stocks even when they didn't even exist in the warehouse. Now he would borrow funds against those falsely inflated inventories for the period of 15 days. For showing interest in repayment, the plant owner would pay some amount knowing that he will get back the paid amount and more, as soon as the new contract will be made. The plant owner would make the investor believe that he has added the said amount of commodity to the warehouse by providing fake warehouse receipts, leading to an inflated commodity; this whole game was Ponzi in nature.

Subsequently, Mr. Rathore noticed that exchange did nothing in the context of the borrowers even when they had poor balance sheets and couldn't even afford the large loans. These borrowers had loans to the tune of INR 12 Billion. The borrowers actually were providing fake warehouse receipts showing the investors that they were investing in new contracts.

Actions Taken by the Regulators:

The regulatory authority for ISCE was Forward Market Commission (FMC) and Department of Consumer affairs (DCA). The regulations for all the forward contracts were controlled by FMC and when they failed in doing so, then the Department of Consumer Affairs acted as a regulator. The situation was reported in April 2012 but ISCE did not take any action; subsequently, a notice from FMC stopped all operations at ISCE. All the contracts of T+25 or T+35 were cut to T+10 on 16th July 2013. This led to rolling over of positions i.e. from one trade per month to three trades per month. Each of the trades had a transaction cost because of which some investors did not roll over position; this type of attitude of the investors lead to the shuttering of the ISCE. The borrowers could neither pay back the money nor had the goods to back it up when they were told to do so. FMC had put a ban on the trading on the stock exchange by the 24 borrowers who were defaulters. As a result of Mr. Rathore's investigation; Mr. Chiranjeev Iyer, the promoter of ISCE was charged with insider trading in ISCE and IMCEL.

CURRENT CHALLENGES

The ISCE scam in 2013 had again questioned the efficiency of commodity markets. Investigations by FMC led by Mr. Rathore showed that the suspension of trading and pay out issues had been because of the systematic failures and certain loopholes in the regulations of the financial markets. Mr. Rathore is still investigating on an unsolved issue whether this scam ensued because of the loopholes in the system or it had been plotted on the basis of Ponzi schemes? The case that Mr. Rathore has at hand gives an edge to discuss the reasons behind this kind of scam. Among few challenges that Mr. Rathore found on the part of FMC as a regulatory body is that "how investors can be prevented from such scams or the Ponzi schemes which had been fatal to them". Resolving this dilemma, Mr. Rathore also sees the importance of investor's awareness about the invested instruments. The biggest problem of recovering money of the investors from the default borrowers is still unsolved for Mr. Rathore.

Questions for Discussion

1. Discuss the role of brokers, promoters, regulators at ISCE.
2. Discuss the loopholes at management level, which led to ISCE Scam.
3. What types of measures should be taken in order to prevent scams like ISCE?
4. How was ISCE allowed to not adhere to the demutualization rule?
5. "If ISCE was incorporated in order to create a platform for the scam with the help of a Ponzi scheme or not." Discuss
6. Why investor awareness programs are important and should be part of financial literacy?

REFERENCES

National Spot Exchange scam derailed commodity market in 2013. (2013, 25 December). Retrieved November 4, 2015, from http://www.businesstoday.in/topics/year-2013:-roundup/2013-flashback-national-spot-exchange-dents-commodity-market/story/201769.html

NSEL crisis: Jignesh Shah proposes haircut to reluctant investors. (2013, 24 August). Retrieved October 29, 2015, from http://www.commodityonline.com/news/NSEL-crisis-jignesh-shah-proposes-haircut-to-reluctantinvestors-56051-1-56052.html

NSEL crisis: RBI says no single promoter should control any exchange. (2013, December). Retrieved October 25, 2015, from http://www.thehindubusinessline.com/markets/commodities/NSEL-crisis-rbi-says-no-single-promotershould-control-any-exchange/article5518719.ece

NSEL scam derailed commodity mkt in 2013. (2013, 25 December). Retrieved October 28, 2015, from http://www.business-standard.com/article/markets/NSEL-scam-derailed-commodity-mkt-in-2013-113122500381_1.html

Pushpa, B.V. & Deepak, R. (2013). An Insight into NSEL Scam. *IOSR Journal of Business and Management, 3(29)*, 18-22.

Shenoy, D. (n.d.). *More NSEL: Just 85 Lakh in Settlement Guarantee Fund.* Retrieved November 4, 2015, from http://capitalmind.in/2013/09/more-NSEL-just-85-lakh-in-settlement-guarantee-fund/

Shenoy, D. (2013, 23 September). *NSEL: The 5,500-crore Scam No One Wants to Deal With.* Retrieved October 29, 2015, from http://capitalmind.in/2013/09/NSEL-the-5500-crore-scam-no-one-wants-to-deal-with/

Shenoy, D. (2013, 4 August). *The Deeper Questions on the NSEL crisis.* Retrieved October 29, 2015, from http://capitalmind.in/2013/08/the-deeper-questions-on-the-NSEL-crisis/

Subramaniam, N.S. (2013, 15 August). *NSEL crisis: Time for Sebi to take leadership'.* Retrieved October 28, 2015, from http://www.business-standard.com/article/specials/NSEL-crisis-time-for-sebi-to-take-leadership-113081500630_1.html

ANNEXURE

Exhibit 1: Borrowers with outstanding amount

Sl. No.	Name of the Borrowers	Total Outstanding Amount (M)	Amount Paid (M)	Net Outstanding Amount (M)
1	PILLAI MINMET INDIA PVT LTD	464.7	30.2	434.5
2	K.N. IMPORTS PVT LTD	9194.2	0.5	9193.7
3	PRABHU PROJECTS LTD.	7702	10	7692
4	THEVAN CONTINENTAL FOOD LTD	3862.1	85	3777.1
5	THEVAN HEALTH FOODS LTD	2944.8	70	2874.8
6	THEVAN OVERSEAS FOODS LTD	861.9	10.8	851.1
7	ROSE REFINERIES PVT LTD	7525.6	0.8	7524.8
8	METAL ALLOYS & IND. LTD.	4142.8	192	3950.8
9	MANIRAJ INDIA PVT LTD	5000.8	520	4480.8
10	SHET FOOD PROCESSING	100.5	12.3	88.2
11	D.N. PROTEINS LTD	9998.9	174.8	9824.1
12	REDDY FOOD INT. PVT LTD	530.7	20.5	510.2
13	REDDY RICE & GEN. MILLS	107.5	3.6	103.9
14	T.P. SUGARS LIMITED	588.5	50	538.5
15	I.N. AGROPROCESSORS PVT LTD	6445.5	129.6	6315.9
16	RAO INVESTMENTS	177.4	72.3	105.1
17	MANIKANDAN TRADING CO	353.4	7.5	345.9
18	COTTON YARN TEXTILES PVT LTD	1382.6	-	1382.6
19	MATANGA OVERSEAS CORP.	1029.8	94.4	935.4
20	RAMESHWAR ENTERPRISES PVT. LTD.	3330.1	-	3330.1
21	THEVAR STLS & PWR PVT. LTD.	1880.1	1752.5	127.6
22	S.V. AGROTECH LIMITED	140.2	0.8	139.4
23	BLUE WATER FOODS PVT LTD	861.2	13	848.2
24	MENON ASSOCIATES	4246.4	190.4	4056
	TOTAL	72871.7	3441.1	69430.7

Exhibit 2: Commodities Present in Various Warehouses

Name of the Buyer	Commodity/ Collateral	Quantity in MT	Warehouse Locations
Rose Refineries	Refined Palmolein oil	4586	Karnataka
Cotton Yarn Textiles	Cotton	4137	Karnataka
T P Sugars	Sugar	17055	Karnataka
Metal Alloys & Industries	Ferro Chrome	23074	Karnataka
Rao Investment	Red Chillies	1667	Karnataka
Shet Food Processing	Paddy	8993	Karnataka
Prabhu Projects	Steel	65250	Karnataka
Maniraj India	Sugar	216334	Telangana
Rameshwar Enterprises	Sugar	110792	Telangana
Matanga Overseas Corporation	Castor Seed	28625	Kerala
D N Proteins	Castor Oil/Castor seed/ Cotton Wash oil	7553/ 96581/ 84766	Kerala
Menon Associates	Sugar	143764	Tamil Nadu
Reddy Food International	Paddy	18870	Tamil Nadu
I.N. Agroprocessors	Paddy	183090	Tamil Nadu
Reddy Rice &General Mills	Paddy	3795	Tamil Nadu
Thevar Steels & Powers	HR Coils	46292	Kerala
Thevan Health Foods	Paddy	225835	Kerala

SECTION

Real Estate

CHAPTER 11

India at Crossroads: FDI Opportunities in Real Estate

EXECUTIVE SUMMARY

India is one of the fast growing major economies of the world. Real estate forms a very important part of the Indian economy. It contributes to about 6.3% of its GDP and provides employment to more than 7.6 million people (CBRE & CREDIA, 2013). In 2005 the Government of India permitted 100% foreign direct investment (FDI) under automatic route in real estate development. This opened a new source of capital and has since played an important role in organised and transparent development of this sector. This case-study traces the evolution of foreign direct investment (FDI) and institutional investment in Indian real estate sector and evaluates resultant opportunities. It further assesses various government actions and policies impacting this sector, market risks and possible pit-falls for international investors in this sector.

Keywords: India, Real Estate, Foreign Direct Investment (FDI), Investment, International Investment

ASHISH GUPTA

Ashish Gupta is an Associate Professor at School of Real Estate, RICS School of Built Environment, Amity University, Noida. He has over 15 years of multidisciplinary experience in academics and real estate industry. He has worked with Jones Lang LaSalle Meghraj in Consulting, Investments and Capital Markets. Subsequently he headed real estate practice within wealth management setup for Bajaj Capital and Aditya Birla Money.

He has Bachelor's Degree in Architecture from Lucknow University, Post Graduate Diploma in Planning from CEPT, Ahmedabad and Post Graduate Diploma in Financial Management from Narsee Monjee Institute of Management Studies, Mumbai.

Recent publications

Gupta, A. & Tiwari, P., 2016. Investment risk scoring model for commercial properties in India. *Journal of Property Investment & Finance*, 34(2), pp.156–171.

SETTING THE STAGE

Vijay, an investment banker works with a leading International Property Consultancy (IPC) in India. During the last few weeks he had met some big investors looking at investments in Indian real estate. This morning he met with the delegation of one of the large pension funds[1] based out of North America during a breakfast meeting at Taj Man Singh Hotel, New Delhi. They had a large investment portfolio in real estate across the Globe and had been keenly watching the Indian real estate market for a few years now. With election of a stable, proactive and reform oriented national government, they had renewed interest in Indian real estate. Vijay presented to them a brief snapshot of the Indian real estate sector and its evolution in the last decade. They were convinced about India's growth story and commissioned him to provide a report on market scenario and investment opportunities. Vijay asked his team to prepare an in-depth analysis of real estate sector, investment trends, critical issues and opportunities to be shared with them.

BACKGROUND - INDIAN ECONOMY AND REAL ESTATE

India is one of the most attractive global real estate markets on account of its fast growing economy, large "middle income group", rapid urbanisation and demographic advantage of having second largest population in the world (1210 million (urban – 377 million)). Indian Gross Domestic Product (GDP) grew by 7.3% during financial year 2015, which was about 0.4% higher than previous fiscal's growth of 6.9%. This stabilisation and growth in economy is in spite of volatility and uncertainty experienced in many major pockets across the globe. In the first quarter ending March 2015, Indian economy grew at 7.5%. This growth is supported by corresponding growth of 11.5% in finance, insurance and real estate services sector and 7.1% in manufacturing (CBRE, 2015). Real estate forms a very important part of the Indian economy and by one estimate contributes 6.3% to Indian GDP and provided employment to more than 7.6 million people in 2013. This contribution to GDP is expected to increase to about 13% by 2025 and employment is expected to increase to 17 million (CBRE & CREDIA, 2013). Since opening of the real estate sector to foreign direct investment (FDI) in 2005, circa 25.3 billion USD private equity has been invested in Indian real estate between 2005 -15 (JLL, 2015).

Indian real estate market is getting organized with FDI and institutional money chasing income generating leased assets. This demand will further get augmented with the introduction of Real Estate Investment Trust[2] (REIT) in India. It is estimated that there was about 169 million square feet of office stock by the end of year 2013, which meets

---

[1]   Pension funds globally are large intuitional investors investing in all major assets classes having a portfolio of over 33 trillion USD under assets. They in developed markets typically invest 5-10% of their portfolio in real estate (APREA, 2014a).

[2]   REIT is a globally accepted investment vehicle listed on stock markets offering common shares to pubic for investment in real estate. It is an extremely liquid instrument to invest in real estate and pay high dividends to investors. REITs have a market worth of over US$ 140 billion in Asia (APERA, 2014b).

FDI investment criteria as per Press Note 2 and 3 issued by Department of Industrial Policy & Promotions, Government of India (JLL, 2014a).

As indicated in Global real estate transparency index 2014 (JLL, 2014b), Indian cities have a ranking of 42-50 i.e. semi- transparent in the list of 102 global markets studied for their transparency. Semi-transparent nature of Indian real estate markets further shows the importance of risk assessment and effective property fund management for institutional investors (example: pension funds, sovereign funds) waiting to invest in Indian real estate.

A Brief History of Institutional Investment in Indian Real Estate

Historically real estate development in India was funded by high net-worth Individuals (HNIs) for buying land and pre-construction activities. This mode of unstructured financing had been both in form of debt and equity. Subsequently construction was self-financed through sales and pre-sales proceeds. Traditionally debt was available from nationalized banks for purchase of land, but subsequently Reserve Bank of India (RBI) restricted debt for purchase of land. Post 2005 with permitting of FDI in development in India, private equity became an alternate source of funding for land and project acquisition.

The beginning (2005 – 2008) - Indian fund management industry started in 2005 with government allowing FDI in real estate. In this period, many global financial institutions invested their balance sheet money in many development projects in India, followed by fund raising for their third party fund management business from global limited partners (LP[3]). Large global financial institutions like Morgan Stanley, Goldman Sachs, Citigroup, AIG, Meryl Lynch, and Wachovia invested money with unlisted developers for portfolio diversification and creation. Promoter cash outs were fairly common, most of these investments were equity investments with structures to protect downward risk. Many domestic financial institutions like HDFC, ICICI, Kotak and IL&FS also raised domestic and/or global capital. Most of this capital focused on high risk and high return opportunistic[4] strategy in real estate development projects.

---

[3]   The investors in private equity fund are called Limited Partners (LPs). They have limited liability in the fund to the extent of their ownership and do not have management responsibilities. These LPs are generally pension funds, institutional investors and wealthy individuals.

[4]   Investment in Greenfield development, this is high risk and high return strategy having development risk and potential of high returns of 20% +.

Post Global Financial Crisis (GFC[5]) (2009 – 2013)

Private Equity (PE) canvas saw disappearance of many of these big players. Project underwriting assumptions by fund managers and land bank valuation standards adopted by property valuers, developers and fund managers also underwent transformation. Investment preference shifted to secure and demand driven self-liquidating residential sector, with PE investments getting structured as debt then pure equity instruments. During this period global fund raising was not very successful, however domestic funds like ABRE, Indiareit, Kotak, Milestone and ASK were successful raising HNI money through private wealth channels.

(Post 2013 - 2016)

Last few years have seen many large global investors, pension and sovereign funds having global portfolio of core assets (stabilized income producing properties) like Blackstone, Brookfeild, CPPIB[6], QIA[7] and GIC [8] acquiring office property portfolio in India in anticipation of entry of REITs[9] in Indian market. Recently government has further eased restrictions on FDI investment through direct route in real estate by removing conditions such as minimum area restriction for development.

CURRENT CHALLENGES FACING INDIA REAL ESTATE SECTOR

Real estate is a capital intensive sector requiring expertise in various fields throughout its life cycle. Enabling environment and transparency can ensure flow of FDI and institutional capital to real estate sector. Indian markets are complex and the last decade has seen extreme volatility with ups and down in investment sentiments. In many cases due to corporate governance, transparency and regulatory issues, many investors have suffered losses. A few of the issues facing the sector include

1. Most of the Indian developers have a poor track record in terms of corporate governance. Traditionally real estate development in India was run like a family business with limited accountability to various stakeholders. The last decade has

---

5   Financial crisis of 2007-08 is also called as global financial crisis and is compared with great depression of 1930s. It started with global credit crunch due to loss in value of subprime mortgages sold by global financial institutions originating from United States.

6   Canada Pension Plan Investment Board

7   Qatar Investment Authority

8   GIC Private Limited, is a sovereign wealth fund established by the Government of Singapore

9   Real Estate Investment Trusts (REITs) are entities that own income generating properties they have participation from retail investors and are listed on stock exchanges.

seen entry of many diversified Indian business houses[10] in property development. This has brought transparency, accountability and professionalism in this sector for the first time. These new entrants enjoy good reputation with the existing investors and have strong credentials to attract institutional capital.

2. There is a large trust deficit amongst the consumers due to developer default in keeping their commitments like timely delivery, price escalation, not paying penalties on delayed projects, increase in super area at the time possession, etc.

3. As per Government of India's estimate there is shortage of about 18.78[11] million houses in urban India in affordable segment. There are many bottlenecks in providing supply of affordable housing like lack of cheap land within suitable travel distances, limited access to home finance for low income groups and high taxation making this segment un-attractive for developers. Proactive government intervention and support can open affordable housing market for end users, developers and investors.

4. There are over 40 approvals needed from various state and central departments for real estate developments. This results in uncertainty in development process in terms of time and cost escalation. Government should bring transparency in project approvals and streamline its regulatory regime to make this sector attractive to the foreign investors.

5. For real estate and infrastructure development land acquisition[12] has become a big issue in India. Modification to the present land acquisition bill is desired by the industry.

GOVERNMENT ACTION TO REJUVENATE URBAN SECTOR AND HOUSING

Government of India, in order to rejuvenate the sector has taken multiple initiatives, RBI has cut repo rate in 2015 by 125 basis points to 6.75%. This rate cut would sooner or later be passed to the end customer by Banks and Housing Finance Companies (HFC), in the form of reduction in home loan rate. This is likely to improve sentiment in otherwise depressed residential property market.

Prime Minister Mr. Narendra Modi after assuming office has launched many initiatives to push urban, housing and property markets' growth by launching:

1. Smart City Mission to develop 100 smart cities across India.

---

[10] Diversified business conglomerates like Tata, Birla, Godrej, Mahindra, Indiabulls and Dabur having interests in financial services, automobiles, telecom, agro products, Information technologies and enabling services (ITES) and manufacturing.

[11] Report of the Technical Urban Group (TG-12) on Urban Housing Shortage 2012-17, Ministry of Housing and Urban Poverty Alleviation, September 2012

[12] In 2013 the then government passed a new land acquisition bill called "The Right to Fair Compensation and Transparency Land Acquisition, Resettlement and Rehabilitation Bill, 2013". This new bill has made land acquisition more expensive and very difficult to acquire new land parcels for development.

2. "Atal Mission" for Rejuvenation and Urban Transformation (AMRUT) for improvement in cities with an outlay of INR 500 billion. This will rejuvenate and provide impetus to augmentation of infrastructure across the country.
3. "Pradhan Mantri Awas Yojana" or commonly known as "Housing for All - 2022", to facilitate delivery of affordable housing in India.
4. There has been substantial progress in implementation of REIT in India. It is estimated that REITs would have 80-100 million square feet asset under management in first three years of their implementation in India valuing about 15-20 Billion USD (KPMG and IVCA, 2014).

Government has shown commitment to policy level initiatives to improve the transparency and sustained growth in real estate and housing by showing its commitment towards policy initiatives like

1. Real Estate Regulatory Bill (RERB) will bring transparency and corporate governance in Indian real estate industry by formation of real estate regulator across various states to regulate this sector. Regulator will monitor developers for their contractual promises, timely possession, project approvals, advertised claims and promises and to ensure that customer's money is used for project completion.
2. Modification in Land Acquisition Bill of 2013 (pending in Parliament), to ensure just and timely availability of land for urban and industrial development.

These steps are critical to ensure housing for all by 2022 and development of 100 smart cities in India, which will need large amount of foreign investment in infrastructure and real estate development.

RECOMMENDATIONS FOR INVESTORS

Looking at various opportunities in this sector Vijay and his team conducted a SWOT analysis of Indian real estate market.

Strengths

1. Indian economy is one of the fastest growing economies of the world which should have positive trickle-down effect on property markets in medium to long term.
2. Strong economic growth has resulted in strong growth in commercial real estate.
3. India has sound demand side basics due to a large middle income group, rapid urbanisation and demographic advantage.
4. Proactive, reform and development focused agenda of a stable central government.

Weaknesses

1. Corporate governance issues with many Indian developers.
2. Transparency issues in real estate market as a whole.
3. Unethical practices of developers have resulted in trust deficit of consumers from the sector.
4. This has resulted in weak market sentiment in residential segment.

Opportunities

1. Robust economic growth and strong demand have attracted many global investors. Global capital can further help local partners by introducing them to best international practices, which in turn will help them gain better market share.
2. International investors can partner with Indian developers having strong corporate governance and timely project completion track record to mitigate local country risk.
3. Investor can participate in infrastructure and affordable housing projects that would need long term capital with low risk and stable return.

Threats

1. Market transparency and corporate governance issues may put investor capital at risk.
2. Slow pace of reforms may result in poor market performance.
3. Poor global economic environment may have negative impact on Indian markets as well.

Vijay based on his study of Indian property markets and client's investment objective[13], made following recommendations for investment in

1. Long term infrastructure projects, these investments are given favoured treatment by the government and in many cases supported by government guarantees.
2. Affordable housing, by entering in partnership with some reputed Indian developer, having good track record of corporate governance and timely construction. There is a huge demand in this segment and have special initiatives by the government. Investments in this segment can have stable income opportunity in medium to long term for investors.
3. Completed stabilised commercial properties having reputed tenants. These assets can later be transfer to REITs. There are many global investors (like pension funds, sovereign wealth funds and other fund managers) actively buying these properties in India.

---

[13] Pension funds have large pool of capital available for long periods looking for stable and low risk returns.

QUESTIONS FOR DISCUSSION

1. What are the key factors that make India an attractive destination for foreign investors?
2. What are the challenges faced by the foreign investors investing in Indian real estate market?
3. Please elaborate key risks that need careful evaluation by foreign investors investing in an emerging economy like India.

REFERENCES

APREA (2014a), The Increasing Importance of Real Estate for Asian Pension Funds

APREA (2014b), The Impact of REITs on Asian Economies

CBRE, CREDIA, (2013). Assessing the Economic Impact of India's the Real Estate Sector.

CBRE (2015), India Residential, 2015, Q1

CREDIA and CBRE (2013), Assessing the Economic Impact of India's Real Estate Sector

JLL, (2014a), India's Stock of Commercial Real Estate. *The new preference for international and domestic funds.*

JLL, (2014b), Global Real Estate Transparency Index, 2014. *Real Estate Raises the Bar.*

JLL, (2014c), Destination India. A Real Estate Journey for Corporate Occupiers.

JLL (2015), Real Estate Private Equity 3.0

KPMG and NARADCO, (2014). Indian Real Estate - Opening Doors.

KPMG and NAREDCO (2015), Decoding housing for all by 2022

KPMG and IVCA (2014), Destination India – Are we ready for the REITS?

SECTION

Entrepreneurship

CHAPTER 12

Women Entrepreneurs: Nurturing Business

EXECUTIVE SUMMARY

Entrepreneurship is associated with purposeful activity and creation of an organisation. Entrepreneurs are business builders and contribute a major chunk to the economic development of the nation. Women entrepreneurs are supported and encouraged by the government to bring women empowerment and to help them to be economically independent. This is also being speculated as a solution to gender diversity in the corporate workplace, Women are still disproportionately represented in the world's economy and the gender gap continues to exist in social, political and economic spheres.

It is critical to eliminate the gender gaps in political, health, education and other sectors but economic empowerment is equally viewed as a crucial contributing aspect that helps to achieve equality between women and men. Discovering and promoting the entrepreneurial potential of women steers growth and development through innovation and job creation and ensures empowerment.

This case is the life story of Surabhi Paliwal, a 25-year-old MBA graduate who decided to make a difference to the society by producing biodegradable paper cups. She had set up a manufacturing plant, SIP Agro Pack Private Limited (SIPAPPL) in Noida. This case traces her struggles for her business and the path she choose. It also talks about the issues this woman entrepreneur faces with a manufacturing start-up in a male dominated industry. The corporate world leaders today are facing critical challenges in managing organizations and meeting the expectation of the stakeholders. Sustainability is a crucial ingredient for an organization's long-term success. This case study highlights the issues faced in sustenance and survival of a small manufacturing unit in a competitive multi-player industry.

Keywords: Woman Entrepreneurs, Entrepreneurship, Paper cup industry, Operations Management, Manufacturing, Small Business, Work- Life Balance, MSME.

KRITIKA NAGDEV

Kritika is an Assistant Professor at Vivekananda Institute of Professional Studies and has three years of experience in Academia and Industry. She has done her Bachelor in Computer Application from Guru Gobind Singh Indraprastha University, followed by Masters in Commerce in Advanced Marketing from University of Pune. Her credentials also include Post Graduate Diploma in Management with specialization in International Business from Balaji Institute of International Business, Pune.

Her research areas are Branding, Service Marketing and E-Banking and her teaching interests are Marketing, Business Strategies & policies, Service marketing, Branding, Marketing Research, and International Business.

SURABHI PALIWAL

Surabhi in an Entrepreneur and has established a manufacturing firm in Noida, Uttar Pradesh producing disposable eco-friendly items such as paper cups, plates, paper napkins etc. that are recyclable and non-polluting in nature. She has done MBA specializing in International Business and Human Resources from Amity International Business School, Noida. She has four years of experience in this sector and her vision is to substitute the harmful plastic products with eco-friendly alternatives and supporting sustainability initiatives.

She also has written articles for Times of India Ascent, Human Capital magazine, People Matters, Huffington Post, elearningindustry.com etc.

SETTING THE STAGE

Surabhi Paliwal was born in Kanpur and grew up in Delhi, NCR. Her father was a businessman, manufacturing gears and machinery parts. Her childhood was spent studying in one of the government schools of Kanpur with her two siblings. Her mother instilled in them good values and wanted her children to do well. She supported her children against all odds and wanted them to focus on their studies rather than learning household chores.

Surabhi was very dedicated and focused on her education. She joined a renowned management institute and pursued her masters in International Business with the help of scholarships and financial loans.

One afternoon, Surabhi was relaxing in a cafe and sipping coffee from a paper cup, waiting for her friends to arrive. Her friends were stuck in traffic and she consumed three cups of coffee, one after the other waiting for them. Surabhi glanced around, people were enjoying their tea and coffee in charming little paper cups. She was amused by the demand of such a simple commodity. Soon, her friends arrived; she joined them and yet kept wondering about this small but important commodity. That was when the idea of SIP Agro pack struck her and she tried to gauge what resources would be needed. Moreover, she was in a dilemma that how she would make her presence felt in the male-dominated manufacturing industry.

JOURNEY OF SIP AGRO PACK LIMITED

Surabhi was the topper of her batch but for her success meant having an opportunity to apply her knowledge of business, learnt from her father and the management degree. This initiated the journey of a small individual firm started by an ambitious young woman. She wanted to realize her dreams and vision of being financially independent and achieve echelons of success.

Surabhi was determined about her business idea. She had started researching the existing suppliers of cups and even started looking for the process of manufacturing paper cups. She went with her idea to her father and teachers to discuss the prospects of paper cup business. Through advice and suggestions, she gained confidence for her venture.

The support of her parents and teachers gave her faith despite the negative and non-supportive attitude of some of her relatives who felt that women are not made for business. They suggested her to go for a salaried job which would have fixed salary and no risks involved. The opposition she faced only strengthened her resolve. She became even more determined to attain success reassuring herself to not be disheartened by such thoughts. She had always believed that one must handle eventualities of life and overcome all hindrances.

Under her father's guidance, she was learning the nuances of business. After about a year, she decided it was time to lay the foundation of SIP Agro Pack Pvt. Ltd. to manufacture biodegradable paper cups which would be of certified quality. This venture was set up thinking that her small initiative would be the first step towards fulfilling her dreams.

During process of registration, Surabhi had found out about numerous initiatives by the central and state governments encouraging and supporting female entrepreneurs.

She decided to get help and support from Trade Related Entrepreneurship Assistance and Development (TREAD) Scheme for Women, a scheme run by Ministry of Micro, Small & Medium Enterprises of Government of India. Guidance related to registration of business, training, finance related issues were provided by the counsellors of Ministry of Micro, Small & Medium Enterprises.

The foundation of SIP Agro Pack Pvt. Ltd. (SIPAPPL) was laid in 2012 in Sector-4, Noida, Uttar Pradesh dealing in manufacturing and supply of biodegradable disposable paper cups. This was set up as the sister concern of Vinayak Ultra Flex Pvt. Ltd. based in Kanpur, Uttar Pradesh dealing in flexible packaging with an annual turnover of more than 25 INR million.

She was overwhelmed to see her dream becoming a reality. Situated on a 250 square meters plot, it had its humble beginning with two previously owned paper cup manufacturing machines. Months later, SIPAPPL had 5 paper cup manufacturing machines in total and a combined workforce of 50 permanent and contract workers. The paper cups were made out of finest food grade paper of 170 to 300 GSM and were Elemental Chlorine Free (ECF). It was certified by ITC Paper Division and was hygienically made at the production unit. The company started delivering their products all over Delhi NCR. The products were appreciated for their quality and beauty of the design. All this was managed by Surabhi single-handedly. The products were produced and developed as per the customized requirements of the clients mentioning the shape, size and design but she gave personal distinctive visual appeal to the cups. This made the innovative designs all the more appealing to the customers. She also gave suggestions about lucrative schemes and strategies to her clients as value addition.

Surabhi aimed to cater to the basic need of quality at economical prices. The company's mission was- 'To manufacture quality with perfect customization ensuring customer satisfaction'. For SIPAPPL budget numbers and timelines were not moving targets; they were the coherent foundation for business functioning. They had experience in areas such as cups/containers for coffee to go, cold drinks, vending, sampling, retail, and portion containers. SIPAPPL took great pride in supporting sustainability initiatives and the reduction of the carbon footprint, with SIPAPPL's vision- 'To ensure that people SIP in quality and to emerge as one of the leading eco- friendly paper cup manufacturers nationally'. She was becoming aware of latest market trends, technology and machines thus was able to manufacture a lot of high-quality items under hygienic conditions. She ensured hassle free and efficient production process with the help of her team of experienced professionals. SIPAPPL's technology was at par with international standards and its talented team of professionals made it a premier player in the paper cup industry. The unit had a sophisticated manufacturing plant, which was equipped with all the advanced machines, equipment, tools and experts.

For delivering value to customers she kept in mind the following checkpoints:

Hygiene factor: SIPAPPL believed in implementing manufacturing process control and quality assurance, which are elements of a quality management system. They had an in-house lab which was equipped with modern instruments required to test for leakage, odour and pasting. They practiced a 5-step testing to ensure quality product. Other than this, the company also got periodical tests done at certified labs for the overall manufacturing of paper cups.

Quality: SIPAPPL believed that quality was a comprehensive aspect and should be ingrained at every stage from raw materials to processes and finally in the final product. They followed rigid quality control procedures, from the raw material stage to the packing stage. The main focus was on offering outstanding products to its customers and sticking to timely delivery schedules. They also had the expertise and capability to execute the bulk order and customized orders as per the buyer's demand.

Social responsibilities: SIPAPPL believed that progress must be achieved in harmony with the environment. A commitment to community welfare and environmental protection was an integral part of the corporate vision.

Production capacity: They had an assortment of Chinese and Indian machines with a production capacity of 4 million paper cups/month. In addition, by using quality raw materials and carefully controlled processing parameters, the trained workers maintained standard practices. These purity levels enabled product specifications previously unavailable in the industry.

The process of production started from the supply of paper from the supplier after it was received in the unit. It was weighed and then sent to the printer for printing. From the printer, it was further sent to the die-cutter, where it was cut in the shape of a 'Blanca' (glass-shape). The Blanca was brought back to the plant and it was placed in the cup making machines where the final product was made. The cups were then packed according to the standard packaging.

Storage capacity: SIPAPPL had a warehouse capacity of 30 metric tons, with proper shelving and high safety measures that helped in maintaining quality and hygiene in all conditions.

CHALLENGES FACED

SOCIAL STIGMA FACED BY WOMEN ENTREPRENEURS

Countries with most successful female entrepreneurs as of March 2015 are India (49%), Hong Kong (45%), and France (42%). Yet in India, the general mind-set of people is that women are suitable for women-oriented products only i.e., clothing, designing, fashion, jewels, and food related dealing business. There were no problems to register and set up her business apart from facing the mind-set against women entrepreneurs trying to set up a manufacturing plant.

CONCERN FOR PRODUCTION

Surabhi had opted for a manufacturing business, which had its associated issues. The major issue was poor production which was a direct result of her lack of skills to manage labor and operations.

Labour management issues

Labour turnover and absenteeism were the critical reasons. In such situations of labour shortage, new workers were hired, who at times did not know how to operate the machines. The inadequacies of knowledge of the newly hired labour further led to machine breakdowns and higher rejection rates.

Operation management issues

The production problems increased due to delays in the processing. Raw material procurement, machine breakdowns and few other reasons were a major cause for delay in the production.

The paper as a part of job work was sent to printer and then a die-cutter for printing and cutting into a glass shape respectively. A delay in this process further caused a setback in the production schedules and hence she was sometimes unable to complete the client orders on time.

The plant had 5 disposable cup making machines each with a capacity of producing 42 cups/minute. The plant ran 12 hours a day and 26 days a month on an average. Hence, the monthly production capacity of the plant was (42 x 60 x 12 x 26) x 5 i.e. 3,931,200 approximately 4 million cups per month. However, the plant was able to produce only approximately 2.8 million a month. Several delays plagued the operations.

One of the factors contributing to the disturbed production schedule was a delay in the raw material supply. The orders were placed keeping the lead time in mind, however, sometimes the paper suppliers ended up delivering late due to transportation issues.

It has been three years for SIPAPPL and Surabhi has been able to build a client base of many corporate clients such as Café Coffee Day, Costa Coffee, Vaango, Max Health Care, India Glycols, IBN7, Kailash Hospital, Birlasoft, Infoedge India, Global Logic, Steria, Fortis Hospital and other catering companies. The multi-retail beverage brands place bulk orders but at the same time expect highest quality at low cost.

These clients have high expectations and require her to be extremely professional in her approach by keeping commitments, delivering on time and also trying to keep costs low without compromising on quality.

With Time comes a Great Responsibility

When she got married in 2015, her commitments increased. She had planned for expansion of her business in that year. Her husband and in-laws were supportive of her decision to carry on with her business. She commuted approximately 60 km daily to manage her home and business. She had several responsibilities on both fronts and she had to constantly balance conflicting priorities.

Fortunately, she got a considerate life partner in Ram Kapoor who understood her emotional attachment to SIPAPPL. He decided to support her in her business. He assisted her with the 'monotonous' side of the business handling labour and keeping accounts. He also helped her in tackling production problems by advance planning, control systems and quality checks. In a way, this support enabled Surabhi to resolve the major problem of labour and operations. This allowed her to focus on innovative designing of cups and strategising for acquiring the untapped market. Thus she was also able to achieve a work-life balance.

Soon the business processes got restructured. SIPAPPL could fulfil orders on time with quality products and at a lowered cost than its competitors. Meanwhile, the second-largest player in the industry - Blanca Mart Agro Limited approached SIPAPPL for a hostile takeover. Blanca Mart was in this business for the last 20 years, capturing a major part of the market. They specialised in the process of production by having best of the machinery for cutting, job-work and for printing as well. Surabhi could sense trouble and out-rightly denied the proposal. This proposal could have paid in millions but she opted to struggle and carve a niche for SIPAPPL.

THE ROAD AHEAD

Surabhi is able to strategize the operations and is trying to acquire new clients. She is working hard for her venture by managing the existing customers, costs and inventory.

She personally checks the quality of batches produced. She feels that it is best to verify every detail. She keeps experimenting with various inputs, sizes, dimensions, shapes and other small things which may get her new clients.

She still dreams of her venture being able to see new heights of success and business expansion is on her mind. Ram has suggested her to apply for FDA (Food & Drug Administration) compliance and export her products to other neighboring countries. Her network of clients could facilitate her getting more deals but expansion means more investment and risk. This would mean an increase in the scale of business to be managed by her. She is in a dilemma to either expand or sustain her existing operations.

QUESTIONS FOR DISCUSSION

1. "Surabhi believed in her instincts to manufacture one of the basic commodities like paper cups." Pen down your views on venturing into this business.
2. Discuss the pros and cons of Entrepreneurship vis-a-vis a Salaried Job.
3. "It's impossible for a women entrepreneur to manage a business as men do." Comment.
4. "Paper cup industry is a competitive industry. Surabhi should have accepted the acquisition deal by Blanca Mart Agro Limited." Suggest your views about takeover and acquisitions.
5. In your opinion, what should be the future goal for SIP Agro Private Limited?

REFERENCES

Bansal, R. (2013). *Follow Every Rainbow*. India: Westland.

Chandwani, J., Bulsara, H.P., & Gandhi, S. (2015). Women Entrepreneurship in India: A Case Study of Jaishree Kabra of Kothari Silk Mills. *International Journal of Business and Management Invention, 4(1)*, 8-13.

Dutta, A. (2015, 8 March). *Nearly half of India's entrepreneurs are women: Study*. Retrieved October 28, 2015, from http://timesofindia.indiatimes.com/india/Nearly-half-of-Indias-entrepreneurs-are-women-Study/articleshow/46489751.cms

Indvik, L. (2010, 18 June). *Starbucks challenges Paper Cup Waste via Sustainability Design Contest*. Retrieved November 8, 2015, from http://mashable.com/2010/06/18/starbucks-betacup-challenge/

Lockrey, S. (2011). The Ecocraze, a Case Study: Negotiating a Greener product design Landscape. *Design Principles and Practices, 5 (4)*, 41-62.

Raghvan, R., & Notaras, M. (2009, 3 March). Sad Demise of Paper Coffee Cup. Retrieved November 8, 2015, from http://ourworld.unu.edu/en/storm-in-a-paper-cup/

SECTION

Marketing/Digital Marketing

CHAPTER 13

Visual Merchandising – Creating a Distinctive Appeal

EXECUTIVE SUMMARY

Visual merchandising, which is a part of shopper marketing, has reached a tipping point. The traditional ways via which companies used to convert shoppers to buyers have become passé. Even though shopper marketing has permeated marketing mainstream only over the last few years it will play a very important role to change the short term tactic of sales promotions to a more strategic discipline that plays a key role in an integrated marketing approach. With an influx of new communication and information media, consumers are rapidly adapting themselves and brands need to quickly understand the shopper behaviour. The in–store (inside the store) and out–store (outside the store) integration needs to be seamless. Visual merchandising is the need of the hour for brands. The case analyses the distinct strategies, brands can use to reach out to shoppers. The case takes the example of a company and discusses the various challenges faced. It explores the benefits of using shopper marketing.

Keywords: Visual Merchandising, Category Management, Merchandizing, Modern Retail; Point of Sale (POS), Shopper Behaviour.

HAVISH MADHVAPATY

Havish works as Head – Research with Traverse Strategy Consultants, a research and consulting start up. An MBA Gold Medallist, he started his career with Reckitt Benckiser, post which he worked as a research scholar, and subsequently as an Assistant Professor. During his stint in academics, his academic research work has been published extensively in national and international journals, and he presented his work at leading institutions across the country such as IMT Ghaziabad, IMI New Delhi, IIT Roorkee, JNU etc.

He is a certified Microsoft Office Specialist (MOS) Excel 2013 and VSkills certified Digital Marketing Master.

Presently he leads a team of analysts at Traverse, and spearheads all research work. He has created models for Brand Ranking, CMO Ranking and Experiential Marketing. He has worked on projects for clients from various sectors around the world, including various ministries of GoI.

SETTING THE STAGE

Bhaskar Chaturvedi looked around him in sheer amazement, coupled with anxiousness. Everywhere he saw chaos. There was a cacophony of noises - people chatting noisily and announcements blaring on the public address system. Seemingly oblivious to all this noise – there were consumers merrily pushing around their shopping carts, browsing products, reading labels and adding them to their shopping carts. There were mothers perusing over which brand of baby-food to buy, trying to resist their kids who were trying their best to drag their mothers to the toys section. There were young couples who seemingly had no interest in shopping but were happily strolling through aisles. Then there were the product salesmen from various companies with a huge smile a permanent fixture on their face trying to sell face creams and deodorants to uninterested consumers.

Bhaskar could not believe that he was standing in the middle of one of the largest supermarkets in the heart of Delhi. At this moment with a notebook in one hand and a camera in the other, he wondered how he would ever manage to decipher this ecosystem, let alone succeed in it.

ORGANIZATION BACKGROUND

Excelsior Ltd. was founded by Bhaskar Chaturvedi and Aneesh Vashisht far away from the chaotic shopping isles in which Bhaskar now found himself. Excelsior was established a year ago by the duo in Kuwait, when they were in their final year of MBA. They were Non Resident Indians (NRIs) and were born in Kuwait. Bhaskar's parents worked as research scientists with a pharmaceutical company in India, before the company moved them to Kuwait. Aneesh's parents were Professors at different Universities and had moved to Kuwait to pursue their joint research and had stayed there ever since.

Bhaskar and Aneesh had come up with an idea of a natural energy drink in Kuwait. Interestingly, what started as a simple idea for a business plan competition had slowly consumed all their attention and before they had completed their MBA they registered their firm. They obtained all the necessary permits and NOC's from the authorities and outsourced the manufacturing to a local juice manufacturer. Within no time they were selling products in all major supermarkets in Kuwait and had earned a handsome profit.

Their energy drink was made using ayurvedic ingredients and all the raw materials were sourced from India. Successful in the Kuwait market and aware of the market potential of ayurvedic products in India, they decided to launch their products there. Since they were still a small firm and their products were priced moderately expensive at 1 Kuwaiti Dinar (approx. INR 220) per 250 ml pack, Bhaskar decided to come to India and survey market opportunities.

CASE DESCRIPTION

Bhaskar decided that Excelsior would only focus on metros. Here too they would only focus on large supermarkets in prime locations, where the client base was open to spending 220 rupees on a single-serve energy drink. After some research, they decided to partner with Premium Supermarkets, which had 45 large-sized supermarkets and hypermarkets spread across Delhi, Bangalore, Chennai and Mumbai. Bhaskar came to India and met Varun Seth, Chief Executive Officer, Premium Supermarkets at his National Office in Mumbai.

Sitting outside Varun's office, Bhaskar felt nervous. Clutching on to his laptop which had his PowerPoint presentation, he realized that convincing Varun would not be easy. Bhaskar was prepared for a long conversation, where Varun would negotiate with Bhaskar and not agree easily, considering Indian supermarkets have an excellent equation with the large beverage companies. Shelf space was prime location with every company vying for it and in turn giving considerable premiums to the supermarket. Bhaskar realized he could not offer any of these large incentives.

Bhaskar began his 80 slides presentation but 2 minutes into the presentation Varun signalled him to stop. Fearing the worst, Bhaskar sat down. Varun was very candid and openly shared his thoughts. He loved the idea but also said that the shelf space was already acquired by the large beverage companies. What Varun could do though, was to allow him access to all the various display units in the stores. If Bhaskar could somehow utilize those display units effectively and manage to entice customers, Varun assured he would get Excelsior prime space in the beverage category. Bhaskar was speechless since he had thought this meeting would be a hit or miss. He had not expected this. Up for a challenge though, Bhaskar thanked Varun and said he would need a month's access to various display units in the stores.

CHALLENGE FACED BY BHASKAR

Bhaskar knew the key fundamentals of retail marketing. But standing inside the store, he realized that the assumptions he had about a supermarket did not hold true here. Having lived in Kuwait – and only having travelled to other developed countries in Western Europe, he was used to meticulous store management in supermarkets. While this supermarket was smaller than the average store in Europe or Kuwait, it was still substantially large. Footfall was great; in fact it almost tested the capacity of floor space as customers were shoving each other for space while manoeuvring through the aisles. He realized that to get the attention of these customers, he would need to carefully manage the visibility of his product.

SHOPPER MARKETING AND INSIGHTS

According to Chris Hoyt [1], "Shopper marketing [is] brand marketing in retail environment." The science of shopping is adapting like never before. As modern retail in India expands and brands become conscious about marketing spend, shopper marketing is becoming one of the most sought after areas for consumer packaged goods (CPG) manufacturers and retailers. The potential lies in its ability to gather insights about the shopper and applying the same to influence their purchase decisions.

Shopper marketing challenges the assumption that the shopper and the consumer are the same. A significant factor in the rise of shopper marketing is the availability of high quality data from which insights may be gleaned to help shape strategic plans.

---

[1]   Chris Hoyt – from Consulting Firm Hoyt & Company

Bhaskar had limited access to the retailer data for other beverage companies. Premium Supermarkets collected a huge amount of shopper data but the same was not being analysed to the fullest. He realized that he could find creative ways to reach and entice customers if he analysed this data.

Shopper Insights and Activation

Shopper insights are a valuable asset in business planning. They are necessary to understand the shopping experience including shopper need states, shopping occasions, shopper behaviour in-store, drivers behind the purchase decision at the shelf and reaction patterns to particular in-store stimuli. Shopper insights feed three activation points:

1. Shopper merchandising
2. Shopper marketing
3. Consumer Marketing

Shopper merchandising is defined as enhancement of the shopping experience through category management, which includes plan–o–gram alignment with shopper needs, aisle / store layout, displays, fixtures etc.

Consumer marketing can be broadly defined in terms of product development, packaging communication and pre-store direct to consumer communication and promotion.

Where are shoppers making the decision?

In-store decision (decisions taken after coming to the store) rate is one of the most reliable measures because it is based upon pre and post shopping interviews - what the shopper anticipates purchasing versus what they actually purchase.

Purchases can be classified into four categories:

1. Specifically planned: Purchases the shopper had planned and bought.
2. Generally planned: Purchases the shopper had thought of generically but not bought.
3. Impulse: Purchases the shopper had not thought of but bought on impulse.
4. Substitutes: Purchases the shopper eventually bought, despite planning a different brand.

Bhaskar knew he would have to keep all these types of purchases into account. He knew from his research that in-store decision-making was very high, even in India

Strategy Employed

Bhaskar knew that for shopper marketing to be effective it needs to work with the predispositions people have while shopping.

Bhaskar knew he had to choose between three strategies:

1. Identification: This would ensure that the products are prominently placed, visible and are easy to find.
2. Disruption: As a non-category leader, he could give financial incentives.
3. Enticement: This would encourage shoppers to explore categories they may not have been thinking about when they entered the store. Using factors like store ambience, lighting, layout etc. the shoppers can be encouraged to spend more time browsing.

The Disruption strategy was out of reach for Bhaskar. He therefore chose a combination of Identification and Enticement.

Visual Merchandising and In-Store Visibility

Store layout and design has become crucial. Visual Merchandising is the art of displaying merchandise in a manner that is appealing to the eyes of the customer. Brands use several in-store branding methods. While visual merchandising by itself refers to setting the tone and theme of displays – the actual physical display units are referred to as *visibility aids / visibility assets*. All the branding and point - of - sale (POS) items are uniform with the broader marketing communication plan of the company, which means that the television advertising, outdoor advertising like billboards and ads on social media all are in sync and it is easily identifiable to a customer that it comes from the same brand.

Bhaskar knew that his company would use other marketing efforts too after testing out their products for a few months. He therefore realized the importance of ensuring that the right way to position his energy drink through various mediums in the store.

The factors he had to consider were:

1. Store layout - the interior arrangement of the store.
2. Selling areas - where merchandise is displayed and customers interact with sales personnel.
3. Sales support areas - devoted to customer services, merchandise receiving and distribution, management offices and staff activities.
4. Floor Plan - arrangement of physical space, the positioning of merchandise groups and customer services in the store.
5. Grid Layout - floor plan that has one of core primary (main) aisles running through the store, with secondary (smaller) aisles intersecting with them at right angles.
6. Fixtures - shelves, tables, rods, counters, stands, easels, forms, and platforms on which merchandise is stocked and displayed for sale.

Bhaskar studied all these aspects in the store carefully, and identified key areas where his product would get maximum visibility.

He also decided to use a combination of visibility assets:

1. Four way browsers: Units open from both sides allowing customers to view products.
2. Alligators: Free standing cut-out display.
3. Dump bins: Bins where large quantities of product are kept without arrangement.

4. Floor Stack Units: Stacking cartons on the floor.
5. Floor Standing Units: Display units that can be made from various materials using a combination of colours, imagery etc. Products can be displayed on boards, hooks and prongs.

Hiring of merchandisers for testing

Bhaskar also decided to hire 2 merchandisers who would promote the products. He chose to employ students as paid interns from an MBA college because he knew that they would work hard and also actively engage with prospective customers, ensuring that the customer go for trials. For these trials, Bhaskar had 500 bottles of the energy drink placed. While he realized the importance of asking questions from the customers, he realized that no one would want to fill up a long form. He therefore decided to be present himself and have a quick 2 minute chat with the customers, asking them:

1. Their first impression of product taste and packaging.
2. Their likelihood to purchase this product as an alternate to other energy drinks.
3. Extent to which customers look at nutritional labels when purchasing energy drinks.
4. Occasions when customers consume energy drinks – such as pre / post sports activities, to reenergize in office when feeling lethargic etc.

CONCLUSION

There were several interesting insights that came up after the test run at the store. He realized that customers are very open and enthusiastic about trying an energy drinks made with ayurvedic ingredients. They were concerned about the sugar content of the drink. Customers also said that would happily recommend the drink to others. High price was not a factor but customers wanted to see high visibility of the product everywhere in the store, as well as on various advertising mediums.

Bhaskar was happy with the response and shared all this feedback received with Aneesh. Aneesh was very excited and said that they should launch the product in various supermarkets. Bhaskar felt though that the product should remain exclusive to Premium Supermarkets as they were the largest supermarket in the country. More importantly keeping the product exclusive would only attract customers even more and create an excitement around the product. Aneesh felt they were limiting their opportunities but decided to go ahead with Bhaskar.

QUESTIONS FOR DISCUSSION

1. Was the decision right to keep the product exclusive to Premium Supermarkets?
2. What other options could Bhaskar have considered while in the meeting room with Varun?
3. What is the importance of product visibility and merchandising?
4. What are the possible customer insights that can be gained by observing customers and talking to them, versus asking them to fill a form?

CHAPTER 14

Metamorphosing Medical Marketing

EXECUTIVE SUMMARY

India is the seventh largest country in terms of geographical area and second in terms of population. Over the decades Healthcare Sector in India has been mostly neglected and oral health / dental health even more so. Only in the last two decades oral heath sectors have emerged independently and registered positive growth, possibly due to improved social economic status and increased awareness of the people.

The dental profession in India started way back in 1920 when Dr. R. Ahmed started the first dental college in Kolkata, West Bengal. As per the databases of Dental Council of India, currently there are around 310 recognized dental colleges with the number of passing graduates each year being 25,000 to 30,000. This huge out-flux has made the field highly competitive. Currently the ratio of dentist to general population is 1:250,000 which suggests that more number of dental graduates are required but this does not depict the entire picture. This steep ratio is only in rural areas and drops drastically to the ratio of 1:10,000 in urban areas. This is one of the reasons that 80-90% of the dentists practice in or around the cities.

Private dental clinics run by single owners constitute about 95% of the total practice. The inflow of corporates into dentistry has led to developing of dental clinic chains. They work with systemized marketing techniques and create professional looks which make them successful in attracting more patients.

Like every other practice, dentists also have to learn, adapt and implement new ideas and strategies to stay competitive. The case aims to highlight the current trends and specific marketing strategies employed by current practitioners in the medical field.

Keywords: Dentistry in India, Marketing Trends in Dentistry, Dental Manpower Requirement, Corporate Dental Chains, Management in Dental Clinic.

POOJA SHARMA

An academician with an aptitude for teaching, she has been an educationist for more than 10 years. She graduated from the prestigious Manipal Academy of Higher Education, with double post-graduation one in the field of Paediatric Physical Therapy and MBA in Health Care Services. Presently serving as Assistant Professor at Amity University Noida, India, she has published more than 15 research papers in reputed national and international journals. She has been invited as a key note speaker at various national conferences. Presently on the examination panel for various national universities and she is also a part of editorial board and panel reviewer in reputed journals. Pooja has been awarded for presentation at AIIMS, New Delhi.

Dr. Vineet Golchha

Dr. Vineet did his graduation from the prestigious Manipal Academy of Higher Education and completed his post-graduation in Orthodontics and Dentofacial Orthopedics. Presently he is serving as Reader, Department Of Orthodontics at Indraprastha Dental College Ghaziabad, India. He has been doing private practice in the field of orthodontics for the past eight years. He has published more than 10 research papers in reputed national and international journals and is also reviewer in many reputed journals including Angle Orthodontics and IJDR. He was the Assistant Secretary at IDA Conference, Mangalore 2008.

SETTING THE STAGE

Dr. Harsh Agarwal, a graduate in dentistry had a well-established dental clinic. He was facing an uphill task in managing his practice. It had been about six months since the income from the clinic was unable to cater even the fixed expenses. He was facing intense competition from increased number of dental clinics in the surrounding locality.

Unhappy with falling revenues, Dr. Harsh decides to try and find out the challenges other dentists with standalone clinics like him were facing and the strategies they were using to not just survive but to succeed. Dr. Harsh decided to visit dental clinics in the city as a marketing analyst from a new company. He felt this was necessary as the dentists would be hesitant to discuss with a fellow practitioner their marketing strategies.

HEALTH CARE INDUSTRY: A SEA OF OPPORTUNITIES

In a country like India administering policies successfully is a very complex matter. The government had pushed for extensive reforms in the health care industry which resulted in a positive growth in this sector. Due to improved social economic stature and increased awareness together with the combined efforts of the World Health Organization, Dental Council of India and Indian Dental Association. Oral health care sector has seen drastic changes in the recent times.

Many studies point out that India's healthcare expenditure is significantly low when compared to the global, developed economies. Yet due to sustained rapid economic growth the country has been creating increased demand for better healthcare. Healthcare as an industry in India is slowly but positively growing. It is expected to exceed USD 100 billion by 2016 from the current USD 65 billion, and is projected to reach USD 250 billion by 2020.

DENTAL HEALTH – THE MACRO ENVIRONMENT AND CHALLENGES

Studies show that 60-65% of Indian population has dental decay and 50-90% has gum diseases. It is alarming to know that as per current studies, 50% of the population has never visited a dentist. One more factor which cannot be ignored is inequality in distribution of dentists. In rural areas, the dentist to population ratio is very less as compared to urban areas.

The frequency and severity of oral diseases require India to have efficient dental education strategies and systems. The huge market of dental industry in India has also made a remarkable impact on the dental education. Mushrooming dental colleges in the past few years in India has led to unemployment and not enough opportunities for all. The average dentists in India operating out of standalone clinics account for nearly 95% of the Indian market. The dentist himself or herself with some assistance does maximum dental procedures. The cost of treatment is generally customized, as per market scenario and definitely negotiable. Specialists are called for specific procedures as per requirement on appointment basis.

The Real Estate prices have been on a high for a long time now; purchase, rental or lease of properties is very expensive. Moreover most of the dentists want to practice in and around towns or metros where the prices are very high and availability is always limited. Dentist to population ratio is 1:10,000 making it a very competitive business.

Dental Tourism forms 10% of the total medical tourism industry and according to a report by Cygnus Business Consulting and Research, is projected to grow at 30 percent per annum to more than INR 95000 million (USD 179,500) by 2017. The potential size of India's dental market is huge and is expected to become one of the largest single country markets for overseas dental device and materials exporters. The Indian market also presents lucrative and diverse opportunities for exporters with the right products, services and commitment. Less than 10% of the population is covered by health insurance hence role of private dentist definitely is the key one.

The competition is getting tougher day by day due to the introduction of corporate backed chains. The new chains are trying to make the experience more patient-oriented. They are working on an idea to design interiors such that the space does not resemble a typical dental clinic. Some have gone ahead and provided lounges with free Wi-Fi access. Few even have a gaming room with play-stations for entertainment of the children who accompany the patients while they are being tended to by the dentist. These facilities can never be matched by standalone clinics due to lack of funds, space and manpower. The other advantage the corporate dental chains have is that they have a pool of dentists and in-house specialists who are available as per need. Also depending upon the reach, dental clinics can cross-sell dental care to patients from Europe and the United States to get procedures performed in India lowering the patient's total cost of dental care.

CASE DESCRIPTION

Dr. Harsh Agarwal got a degree of Bachelor of Dental Surgery (BDS) after years of dedication towards the subject. After graduating in 2004 he started his dental practice in Noida in Uttar Pradesh, India. Though he belonged to a small town Moradabad, he chose Noida as it was regarded as new hub for industrial growth. With industries being set up, more infrastructure facilities and job opportunities were created, attracting many people to this relatively newer town. High density of population allowed a wider patient base to be established.

His single chair dental clinic was established in a commercial shop of 340 sq. ft. in a market place of sector 50. Being the largest market place nearest to the sectors 40, 41, 50 and 51 the market had a good footfall of customers every day. Dr. Harsh did not have to depend on lot of marketing strategies and the only thing he did was to place a neon sign board at his clinic's entrance. His practice did well from the very first day and his attention to marketing ideas and strategies was minimal.

His clinic was doing well as there were only six clinics in the neighbouring sectors and none of them were centrally located giving him a locational advantage. The inflow of patients was good and with quality treatment provided by him the patient base was widening.

Slowly the scenario took a turn for worse. Many new dental clinics were set up in the neighbourhood in a short period of time. These newer clinics, mostly opening in residential premises used extensive marketing strategies to draw the patients. They were displaying boards, putting up sun-boards and inserting pamphlets in newspapers to create awareness among people. Dr. Harsh was initially reluctant and believed that his practice did not need additional expenditure on marketing.

With each passing year the number of dental clinics increased and there were about 22 dental clinics in the surrounding sectors with four clinics being set-up in the same market. Marketing competition and price war initiated amongst these dental clinics. Each one was trying to outdo the other with huge discounts and even monthly instalment schemes were advertised for patients.

In June 2015 a dental clinic chain acquired a 1200 sq. ft. of prime real estate near his clinic and established their centre. This dental clinic chain had the largest sign boards and advertising banners placed. They went ahead with schemes like family membership and gave huge discounts on dental treatment even marketing their availability as 24 x 7.

Dr. Harsh by now was struggling with his practice as dental clinic chains with better marketing practices were attracting more patients. Price cuts, heavy inaugural discounts and package deals given by these clinics had got them a major chunk of Dr. Harsh's business. Slowly the number of new patients coming to his clinic had reduced and even many of his regular patients had switched to different clinics.

Despite years of clinical experience and expertise he was finding it difficult to survive in the current scenario. The situation was even worse for other newer budding dentist who did not have an established practice. According to a study less than 5% graduated dentists in India are working in the Government sector. Private sector jobs were also limited.

CHALLENGES FACED

On one hand, increase in the number of graduates of dentistry is good for overall oral health of the country; on the other hand, there is growing number of unsatisfied dental graduates mainly because there are very low prospects of a job. Standalone dental clinics are facing tough competition from fellow professionals and growing dental clinic chains. Even after purchase or lease of space the setting up of the clinic requires a lot of expenditure.

Dentistry equipment is expensive. Majority of the equipment has to be imported from Germany, USA and China. Currently the proportion of import is around 85%. Higher import duties make the equipment even more expensive. There are very few Indian manufacturing companies which supply dentistry goods. Though recently companies like 3M, Vivadent, Coltene have opened offices in India, this has however still not brought the prices down.

A major problem faced by the dentists is also the constant increase in the cost of consumables. The overhead charges also increase every year with increase in electricity, water and maintenance bills. On the other hand charges for dental procedures are not increasing due to the increased competition from newly opened clinics in the vicinity targeting the same population base. Though price is not the sole criterion for all patients i.e. patient satisfaction and comfort are other relevant factors but for new patients the treatment price is an important factor affecting the decision. The newly opened dental clinics in order to attract patients give lucrative offers and are even willing to work below the market rate.

Marketing strategies by the clinics like giving a family package, giving summer discounts for students requiring braces treatment or a seasonal discount does attract more patients.

The dental diseases though affecting overall heath is not as debilitating as heart or other systemic problems so majority of patients do not emphasize on quality and sterilization necessity.

In conclusion marketing strategies are definitely playing an important role in drawing patients to a dental centre. There is an ample growth opportunity in the field of oral health care marketing in India. There is a need to effectively identify the challenges and to develop effective ways to overcome them.

QUESTIONS FOR DISCUSSION

1. Discuss the role of marketing research for Dr. Harsh's problem.
2. Identify and discuss the marketing decision problem in this case.
3. What according to you should be the best marketing strategy?
4. What is the scope for fresh dental graduates in the current scenario?
5. What according to you are the current trends in dental practice and how to achieve them?

REFERENCES

Elangovan, S., Allareddy, V., Singh, F., Taneja, P., Karimbux, N. (2010). Indian Dental Education in the New Millennium: Challenges and Opportunities. *Journal of Dental Education, 74(9),* 1011-6.

Indian Dental Market 2010. (n.d.). Retrieved October 16, 2015, from http://www.marketresearch.com/Life-Sciences-c1594/Medical-Devices-c1126/

Jain, H., Agarwal A. (2012). Current Scenario and Crisis Facing Dental College Graduates in India. *Journal of Clinical and Diagnostic Research, 6(1),* 1-4.

Parkash, H., Mathur, V.P., Duggal, R. Jhuraney, B. (2006). Dental workforce issues: A global concern. *Journal of Dental Education, 70(11),* 22-26.

Tandon, S. (2004). Challenges to the oral health workforce in India. *Journal of Dental Education, 68(7),* 28-33.

CHAPTER 15

Digital Marketing: Need and Effective Usage as a Marketing Channel

EXECUTIVE SUMMARY

In times when Entrepreneurship is being supported and encouraged by the government and society alike, entrepreneurs find the buzz words like Digital Marketing, Social Media Marketing appealing. They try to leverage such platforms in any possible manner as it has become the most common and cost effective method of promoting one's organization – profit or otherwise.

This case relates to a new medical clinic establishment, Ruchi Physiotherapy & Rehabilitation Centre, which is now about a year old. The clinic's practitioner, Dr. Ruchi, has been a known face in the locality for her knowledge and skills for more than 15 years. When she embarked on her entrepreneurial journey, she started her own practice instead of continuing at Zeus Hospital, New Delhi as a resident physiotherapist. To promote her clinic, she started with conventional means of marketing. Later she also pursued newer channels of marketing including digital marketing. Since cost played an important factor to move to digital marketing, use of just one of the digital marketing tools alone was not enough. Hence mixed approach was adopted to provide a comprehensive solution and reach the target audience. The change in response rate was very positive and gave an impressive long lasting brand building tool.

This case is a synopsis of a live example where the efficacy of conventional channels of marketing and promotion is further enhanced by utilizing various tools of digital media marketing, depending on the target segments and various other factors – demographic, age and digital literacy.

Keywords: Digital Marketing, Social Media Marketing, Internet Habits, Marketing, Entrepreneurship, Ruchi Physiotherapy & Rehabilitation Centre

AKSHAT GARG

Akshat did his graduation in Electronics and Communication Engineering from Madan Mohan Malaviya Engineering College, Gorakhpur. He did his Master's in Business Administration from Symbiosis, Pune. He has been serving in the IT industry for more than 16 years, primarily leading various engagements in payments modernization space. He has attended various conferences like India Digital Summit and continues to build and share his knowledge through various forums.

SETTING THE STAGE

Dr. Ruchi was once again feeling helpless with the rejection of her proposal to get new state of the art physiotherapy equipment at Zeus Hospital. The hospital was a renowned name in New Delhi for patient care and patients poured in from Delhi and adjoining areas. Doctors like Dr. Ruchi had worked hard to take Zeus Hospital to where it stood today but the hospital management was less than helpful in their endeavour. The doctors were of the opinion that there was better equipment available to cater to specific patient needs, which would also reduce the time and cost of treatment. However, the hospital management was not willing to invest time and money in the infrastructure and disturb the current flow of patients. Moreover, Zeus Hospital had been getting a satisfactory turnover based on the current set up and hence the management did not feel the need to upgrade. They were also satisfied with the performance of the physiotherapy division, based on patient turnout and feedback.

Many of the doctors were dissatisfied with the regressive approach of the management and were thinking of shifting to other hospitals. Dr. Ruchi was one of them but she had a different idea. She had been nurturing a dream of having her own established practice and she knew the time was now.

ORGANIZATION BACKGROUND

Dr. Ruchi had an aim of providing excellent patient care in the field of physiotherapy. During her Master's program, she had been introduced to a new set of therapies which she wanted to implement through new methods and equipment at her clinic. Also, within her peer network and in the medical conferences about physiotherapy, there was always mention of the latest techniques and the need to upgrade to be relevant in the competitive market.

With her life's savings and a lot of determination, Ruchi Physiotherapy & Rehabilitation Centre was started by Dr. Ruchi, in July 2014 at rented premises in Mayur Vihar area of Delhi offering the latest in physiotherapy treatment. She had been a known face in the area for her positive attitude and skill set along-with 15 years of clinical experience. Dr. Ruchi was very confident that the new developments in the field of physiotherapy will be welcomed by the patients and will result in their faster recovery and considerable decrease in medical bills.

CASE DESCRIPTION

Launch marketing for Ruchi Physiotherapy & Rehabilitation Centre was conceptualized with the idea that the maximum patients for physiotherapy are senior citizens and home makers. Hence, conventional methods of advertisement were devised, which included flex boards, hoardings, pamphlets etc. This was complemented by visits to established doctors to apprise them of this new set up of physiotherapy that was coming up in the area, so that they could advise the patients to take advantage of the same.

While this was not a cost-effective solution for a start-up, this seemed to be the most appropriate one. Hence sufficient amount was provisioned, after the cost estimates were taken from relevant vendors. This included working with different vendors for different means to effectively utilize the intended budget. Also, a major share of the overall budget was to be spent on the centre readiness and associated equipment. A corpus of INR 2.5 million was established through savings and borrowing from family which was used primarily for the following three categories:

- Launch marketing - INR 0.6 Million
- Centre readiness / Furnishings – INR 0.8 Million
- Equipment's – INR 1.1 Million

This launch marketing strategy resulted in creating an initial inflow of patients from the area for the clinic along with creating a positive brand for the new clinic. The launch marketing primarily consisted of flex boards across the streets and tele-calling her patients to ensure that they were aware of the new place. Bulk messages were subscribed to be broadcasted. Since Dr. Ruchi had already spent a considerable time in the locality, there was a constant flow of patients. These patients were mostly the satisfied lot from her previous role as an employee at the hospital and were return clients. Table: 1 shows the daily average number of patients attended to, for the first 12 weeks.

Table: 1 Daily average number of patients attended to

Week #	Week 1	Week 2	Week 3	Week 4	Week 5	Week 6	Week 7	Week 8	Week 9	Week 10	Week 11	Week 12
No of Patients	15	12	13	12	14	12	14	13	15	11	12	13

CURRENT CHALLENGES FACING THE ORGANIZATION

The patients were satisfied with the treatment options available and the timely curative effects on their pain. While Dr. Ruchi was largely content with the initial response, there was a need felt to take the advantage of this momentum and grow further. A lot of it can be attributed to the entrepreneurial spirit of the doctor and to make optimal utilization of the equipment and the hired staff. While word-of-mouth communication was initially effective, Dr. Ruchi realized that it was not resulting in significant increase in number of patients visiting the clinic. Over 80% of the patients were either return clients for a different ailment or were approaching the doctor based on the positive feedback from a patient who had earlier come here for a treatment. There was a need to do more to attract newer patients for future growth.

A website www.ruchiphysio.com launched initially, was not getting the intended viewership even though it was being promoted within the premises of the clinic to the visitors, and with laminated printouts. While people appreciated the website of the clinic, they were not talking about it once they stepped outside of the clinic.

SOLUTIONS AND RECOMMENDATIONS

A lot of informal conversations had pointed out to an ever growing need of having a digital presence to boost the line-up at the clinic. Hence a plan was prepared to spread the good word about the clinic through the digital media. It was also realized that the conventional modes were already utilized at the launch and hence the first awareness has already happened. It was felt digital marketing shall be more cost effective as compared to other conventional methods.

Following four options were considered as part of enhancing the Digital presence:

1. Clinic Website: The needful was done to understand the process of redesigning the current website. Also a broad idea of the costs involved for an interactive website – one-time and recurring – was sought. The content was prepared and a student was identified to help with the preparation of the web pages. The costs incurred with the student designer were less as compared to hiring a consultant. There was more focus on the content on the website, so that people visiting the same could use it for comprehensive information.
2. Facebook Page: A Facebook page was created to cater to the growing audience of Facebook savvy people as their single like, could make all their friends also aware of this new clinic and hence help improve patient-base. In-house consultations were done to help with the page readiness and launch.
3. Google Plus: A page of the clinic, similar to the one on Facebook, was created on Google-Plus. This presence also helped during a Google search for listings.
4. Search Engine Optimization and Database Listings: Various search engines like Google, Bing etc. were explored to identify the best value for money. This was the most cost intensive option. Alternative modes of payment were explored and decided based on the best possible outcome. The clinic was also listed on databases like Just Dial, Yellow pages etc.

IMPACT OF DIGITAL MARKETING

The above measures took approximately six weeks to be implemented. The inflow of patients from week 19 onwards was seen increasing, based on the efforts and resources deployed in Digital Marketing.

Graph 1: Inflow of Patients

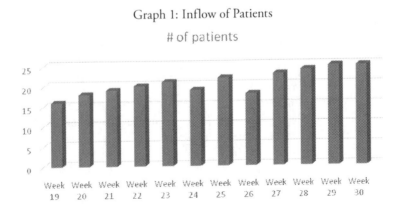

A few interesting points were also noted from the information collected from the patients at the time of registration.

1. 80% of the patients were aged 45 and above, with roughly an equal distribution from a gender perspective. (just 7% more females than males)
2. Nearly all the patients carried a smart phone, but not all had an active mobile data connection.
3. They would usually connect to the internet only at home, using Wi-Fi.
4. While this was also to save costs, another reason was that they needed more time to read and understand (on web page/ app) and hence they found it more convenient to do it at home.
5. They were not regular (daily) for checking updates on social media, but used internet primarily for chatting (WhatsApp) and Skype (video calling with near and dear ones).
6. They paid heed to the content on social media and they spent time reading and understanding the same.
7. Reviews and feedback of others drove them to build an initial trust even before they met the doctor for the first time.
8. Some did seek help from the staff to post online feedback on their behalf after the treatment.
9. More Facebook likes came from patients, who stayed with the younger ones at home. Presence of younger children at home improved digital awareness.
10. This population also liked a few other similar pages to keep them informed.

Conclusion

Depending on the target audience, the digital marketing approach can work either by itself or it can be complemented by the conventional channels of marketing. The strategy has to be devised carefully to gain the maximum response for the establishment. Also the order of the channel of marketing employed becomes important as it that helps to establish the first impression of the organization in the digital world.

Questions for Discussion

1. What are the common challenges faced in an entrepreneurial journey.
2. Discuss the cultural implications of moving from a salary based role to an ownership role.
3. List the methods to leverage digital marketing to achieve a better ROI for a medical start up. What channels to consider for digital marketing.
4. How to improve the marketing content for digital marketing based on the feedback from patients.

REFERENCES

Harrison, J.P. (2010). *Essentials of Strategic Planning in Healthcare.* Chicago, III: Health Administration Press.

Publicity for Business | Marketing MO. (2013). Retrieved from http://www.marketingmo. com/campaigns-execution/publicity-for-business/

SECTION
Human Resources

CHAPTER 16

Talk the Change & Change the Talk

EXECUTIVE SUMMARY

Organizations work in dynamic environment today. Decisions taken by management are often driven by objectives of profitability, cost effectiveness, maximisation of revenue, survival in face of competition etc. At the same time, organizations also need to be sensitive to employees' needs, especially when changes impacting them take place. Organizations that fail to do so often face severe problems such as disruption of production and services, loss of employees, mismanagement of work, to name a few. It is indeed a fine balance that organizations need to achieve and execution of the change determines how successfully it will be implemented.

The present case study narrates the case of one such organization which failed to read the pulse of its employees. It talks about a situation where a significant decision impacting the entire organization was kept under wraps till the last minute, much to the chagrin of its employees. The organization failed to use communication as a powerful tool for managing change. The problems ensuing thereon and the measures taken by the organization to mend the situation further establish that employees are the most important asset that is available to organizations. The value of this asset cannot and should not be undermined under any circumstances.

Keywords: Competency Mapping, Temporary staffing, Communication, Attrition, Training and Development, Leadership, Succession planning, Kurt Lewin's model of Change Management

SHWETA SHRIVASTAVA

Shweta Shrivastava is a Ph.D. Research Scholar at Amity University in the domain of Human Resources. Her interest areas are rewards and incentives, organizational commitment and organizational behaviour. She has seven years of corporate work experience with organizations like Mercer Consulting, Everonn Education and HCL Technologies. She is a Post Graduate in Human Resources from Loyola Institute of Business Administration, Chennai and a Graduate in Commerce from Shri Ram College of Commerce, University of Delhi.

SETTING THE STAGE

On 1st November 2013, management of the organization sat in a meeting room looking at the consolidated exit feedback of almost half the entire employees' strength who had left the organization in the last three months (August, September, and October). The numbers were alarming and the feedback led to a common inference that employees were not happy with the recent shift of the office location. Most of these employees had been employed with the organization since its inception which meant that the loyal employees too were unhappy 'enough' to part ways with the organization. Thus, a Special Assignment Team was created and tasked to chart out a solution plan for the situation at hand. The team was given two weeks to complete the task.

ORGANIZATION BACKGROUND

XY Associates Inc. was a placement agency firm that provided employment solutions to various organizations in Delhi/NCR region. It was established in 2008 and operated with strength of approximately 100 employees. The firm specialised in talent search and acquisition for leadership and mid-level positions, primarily in the Information Technology (IT) and Information Technology Enable Services (ITES) sectors. Slow expansion was the goal of the company with the foray into Legal Process Outsourcing (LPO) and Game Process Outsourcing (GPO) as the next big move. It was doing well and was starting to make a name for itself in the industry for the quality of service it provided to its clients. Its clientele consisted of around 150 mid-sized companies with which it had been consistently engaging in business.

The firm had its only office in the heart of New Delhi- Connaught Place. The convenient and central location of the office and good connectivity through public transport worked favourably for the organization. Amenities and benefits provided to employees were basic and work environment was peaceful. Employees were able to maintain a healthy work life balance and were in general satisfied with their workplace.

CASE DESCRIPTION

Since the past one year, there had been immense pressure on the Management of XY Associates to cut costs in order to maintain profitability. One of the areas that garnered maximum attention in this regard was the burgeoning property costs in the area of Connaught Place. This area was a prime location in the city and housed offices of well-known organizations. Looking at the increase in cost of renting commercial property in this prime business hub of Delhi and in the hope of doing away with some of the pressure of cost cutting, the Management decided that a new office space would be bought in the National Capital Region (NCR). The new office place in Greater Noida, an upcoming commercial and residential location in the NCR, was around 40 kilometres from the office in Connaught Place. It was quoted as well designed and was said to be consisting of 'state-of –the-art' facilities.

The new office was operational from 1st August and employees were informed about it in the last week of June. The implementation was perceived as sudden and the resulting inconvenience led to large number of employees leaving the organization.

General feedback from various business segment heads was that owing to the exit of many employees, they were not aptly staffed to work on client assignments. As a result of this, they were on the verge of losing old clients. Key positions in the organization were lying vacant due to lack of resources. To manage this lack of resources, new employees had been hired but quite a few of them had quit after a short tenure and thus there was no one to manage the fast piling backlog. Consequently, they started missing client deadlines and in general failed to drive the client centric behaviour that XY Associates spoke of proudly.

In a nutshell- business was suffering, employees were unhappy and the situation called for some immediate remedial action. The Special Assignment Team was given a time frame of two weeks to chart out the action plan for bringing the current situation under control.

CURRENT CHALLENGES

The Special Assignment Team had a tough task at hand as they needed to evaluate the reasons that triggered the chain of problems for XY Associates and then provide resolutions. These problems, which had cropped up due to few characteristics inherent to the culture of the organization, have been summarised as below:

COMMUNICATION

Communication forms the backbone of any people based activity (Singh, 2009). Its importance has been stressed upon for the success of organizations. It is the medium through which information is circulated, feedback is taken, policies are communicated etc. In an organizational set up, it is very important that employees are not kept in a black hole where they do not have access to updates of their own organization. In cases where employees are simply asked to complete their tasks and head home, where they are not engaged in the organization, the chances of them feeling disconnected with the organization are very high. This is exactly what happened in the case of XY Associates, especially because most employees had spent long time in the organization and hence expected to be treated as stakeholders in the decision making process.

Management at XY Associates had been contemplating the movement since 2012 but chose to keep it under wraps fearing what eventually happened – loss of resources and disruption of work. This decision was in the knowledge of only the two top leaders and three business heads. The latter had been given instructions that it was not to be shared even with next level employees until all details had been finalised.

CHANGE MANAGEMENT

Alienating employees seemed to be a common practice at XY Associates. Problems for the organization had started on the evening of 20th July when a meeting of Managers had been called and the news was imparted to them. They were asked to cascade the information to their subordinates that XY Associates would operate from the new location with effect from 1st August. It came as a shock to employees who had no inkling about the impending change. They had been given a very short timeframe to react, let alone to plan how they would cope with this change. The obvious question most of them had, was regarding the delay in communication of this information. They were told that it was a 'management decision' and that the new facility was much more state-of-the-art and comfortable as compared to the current one. However, that was hardly a matter of concern for them. Employees were left in the lurch and felt that they had not been treated justly.

This change meant different things for different employees: a possible increase in travel time, a change in the means of transport, change in rental accommodation, time management etc. All this ultimately lead to a ripple effect on their day to day lives as well, requiring them to make changes on personal fronts also. However, the maximum damage was done to employees' faith in the organization. This event eroded the trust that employees had on the organization, its functioning and its value system. They feared that there was no certainty and they could not count on the management to consider their well-being in the long run. Loyalty and their tenure in the organization had no value for the Management. Employees were unsure as to what their future in the organization held for them.

INACCESSIBILITY OF LEADERSHIP

The leadership of XY Associates, like always, was unapproachable and inaccessible for employees. There was no way to communicate with them regarding any issues that they faced due to this decision. The Human Resource team became the "go-to place" for redressal of related queries. However, they were unable to do so due to lack of information or knowledge.

UNAVAILABILITY OF RESOURCES

By the end of October 2013, 22 employees had left the organization after serving the required notice period of 1 month. 8 employees were in the process of exit. While there were many client assignments that needed attention, some 'Critical Accounts' ranked very high on priority due to the high profits associated with them or due to the specialised skill set of the recruiter.

For example, some premium clients of the organization sought incumbents for senior positions or C-Suite positions - such as CEOs, COOs, Managing Directors, Presidents, and Chief Technical Officers etc. Some other assignments depended highly on recruiter's expertise and sound judgement. Exceptional communication skills, an in-depth understanding of position requirements coupled with good judgement of people skills were some of the pre-requisites. Clients were often finicky, choosy and particular about candidates lined up for interviews for these positions.

At XY Associates, there was a separate team of five employees who used to work on such critical accounts. Three of them had left the organization and the task of closing the eight pending assignments was to be completed by remaining two in the next six months. Exit of such recruiters meant that those key skills were not available for taking those important decisions. These were matters of great concern for the Management.

INTERNAL WORK PRESSURE

XY Associates was not prepared or equipped to handle this or other similar crisis. To combat this situation where there was a dearth of experienced resources, new and inexperienced employees were asked to handle critical accounts. In this desperate situation, without any prior actionable plan or intimation to these un-trained employees, key accounts were handed over to them. Exiting employees were asked to train their juniors as a part of their exit process. More so, to extract performance from junior employees, the successful closure of these accounts was included in their performance metrics as well. This created undue and uncalled for pressure on these employees who were not trained or prepared for handling such assignments along with their usual responsibilities. They often had to burn the midnight oil to meet deadlines but were unsuccessful.

FEAR OF LOSING CLIENTELE

As much as XY Associates was trying to make up for missed deadlines, it was worried about its image with its clients. Few clients had expressed their displeasure by withdrawing contracts. The organization had asked for extensions but was having to provide explanations as they were known for their timeliness and quality of work. At the moment, the concern was to not let the internal mismanagement impact their clients.

SOLUTIONS AND RECOMMENDATIONS

The Special Assignment Team envisaged a two staged plan for bringing the situation in order. A short term plan was devised to control the immediate damage and a long term plan was developed to take some strategic initiatives.

The foremost problem that the Management perceived was that XY Associates was not in a position to lose its existing employees and thereby suffer more business loss. Many trained resources had quit, absenteeism was high and people were unhappy. Thus, it was now time to chart out an action plan to restore the faith of employees.

SHORT TERM MEASURES
TWO-TIERED COMMUNICATION PLAN

This was the first step taken by the Management to control the immediate problem. A two -tiered communication plan was created to rebuild connection with employees. Both phases were to be completed by end of February 2014.

Tier 1: Leadership and employee interaction

To attain the congruence of organizational and individual objectives, mission and values, communication should always flow from top to bottom. It also makes the message more credible and motivates employees at all levels. In cases where this is missing, employees tend to feel that they are working in silos and that the management or their leadership does not care about them. This can also lead to employees feeling disconnected with the organization and misalignment between goals of both the entities (Kapoor, 2015). In the long run this can turn out to be harmful for the organization. Regular and well-intended communication positively indicates that leaders in the organization wish to make employees feel involved and engaged. Keeping this in mind, an All Employee

Town Hall meeting was immediately conducted on 10th November by the Managing Director and other leaders to address the employees. Acceptance of the fault of improper and untimely communication was the primary message conveyed by senior management.

Additionally, an open forum was created for employees to raise their issues and to discuss their problems. It helped that the management tried to understand and acknowledge employees' issues. Employees felt that their problems were being addressed and that they were being given a patient ear by the organization. This mellowed their anger and cooled tempers to a great extent.

There were other concrete outcomes of this interaction. Communication framework was made robust. For example, monthly emails were to be sent to all employees to keep them abreast of the business updates, results, upcoming plans, new clients etc. An employee feedback mechanism was set up to pro-actively solicit employees' ideas and opinions about various matters in the organization. They were provided opportunities to voice their opinions, share feedback and also provide suggestions.

Tier 2: Interaction between Human Resources Department and Employees.

Several meetings were held with employees in groups and on one-on-one basis in order to counsel them and to understand their problems. Despite the pressure on management to limit costs, leadership opined that the situation called for immediate measures and hence all support was extended to employees. Implementation was targeted by the end of December and a review of the same was planned a month after that. It was communicated to employees that such meetings would be held regularly in future.

1. Provision of shuttle buses at a very nominal cost from nearest local train station to office to help cut fuel costs of employees
2. Facilitation of car-pools
3. In house meal facility for employees for at least coming 3 months
4. Concierge desk in office premises to assist employees in looking for suitable accommodation close to office
5. Option of flexible working hours once a week
6. "Work from home" facility once a week
7. Over-time payment for longer than scheduled 11 working hours (including 2 hours of commute)

Post implementation of the above mentioned action items - feedback was collected from employees through a survey regarding management's initiatives to normalize employees' work lives and to identify scope for betterment.

WORK MANAGEMENT MEASURES

Loss of business had affected XY Associates in a big way and had to be curtailed immediately. Existing employee base and their skill set was insufficient to handle the work flow. Hence, some ideas were implemented to control the situation.

Temporary staffing was the first step taken to tackle the increasing work load, especially related to critical accounts. Special Assignment team suggested initiating temporary staffing with short-term and close-ended contracts. This way with limited financial resources skilled employees were made available to the organization to meet the urgent needs. Short term contracts of three months were entered into with free-lancer recruiters to provide specialised service in this domain. This helped them tide over the immediate crunch of staff to an extent.

Junior recruiters were aligned to the two experienced recruiters to enable them to learn the job. Instead of handing over the entire job to them, they were asked to assist in activities like initial screening on basis of job description, initiating calling, documentation etc. Also, closing critical accounts and decision making was excluded as a performance measure for junior recruiters. Decision making continued to be managed by senior recruiters.

As a last resort, time concession was sought from existing clients at a reduced cost of services. Business heads were asked to approach their clients and apprise them of the situation at hand. It was reasoned that honesty and transparency in communication would pay off in retaining clients.

In the long term, there were some measures that were needed to be taken in order to make the organization strong and well prepared to meet such unforeseen circumstances. The below mentioned steps were devised in that direction.

LONG TERM MEASURES - STRUCTURED APPROACH TO CHANGE MANAGEMENT

What had triggered the entire chain of events at XY Associates was the poor handling of an important event impacting the entire work force. To make a change successful, it is imperative that it should be planned, communicated and executed with a structured approach. The Special Assignment Team suggested that to manage changes thereon, XY Associates adopt the 'unfreeze, change/transition and refreeze' approach based on the Kurt Lewin's[1] model of change management. This approach helps segment the process of change into three manageable phases and to analyse challenges in each phase proactively.

While the magnitude of a change might vary, change often requires doing things in a new or a different way (Shrivastava, 2014). Mostly, changes which have a direct impact on employees require the maximum adjustment and often prove tough to handle. In each stage of the Lewin model, the HR department should play an important role for the change to be successful owing to its all-encompassing nature. The HR department at XY Associates failed to anticipate the business impact that the change could have on the organization at each of these stages.

'Unfreeze' stage is where employees have to let go of old ways of doing things. Typically, this stage can be easily said to be the most difficult of the entire change process as it requires discontinuing current habits/attitudes and adopting others. Here, it is important that the barriers to change are reduced and that there is a 'felt need' in

---

[1] Change management refers to a structured process of implementing change. A German-American psychologist, Kurt Lewin developed this simple yet practical change management model involving three steps: unfreezing, change/transition, refreezing; using the analogy of changing the shape of a block of ice. Developed in the 1950s, it is one of the cornerstone models for understanding organizational change and is often said to be the foundation of many modern change models.

employees for the new state of affairs (Shrivastava, 2014). Creating that felt need through regular and direct communication with employees is a prerequisite for the Management and the HR department. In the current context, omission of any communication regarding the new location was a miss on the part of management due to which the information was perceived as an instruction rather than a collaborative decision. Top Management and the Human Resources should have charted out a well framed communication plan to convince employees that the movement to new location was a possible solution to the organization's problem.

The state of 'transition is' a very crucial one. Clearly, employees at XY Associates expected to be a part of important events and transitions concerning them. The sudden change was misconstrued as an imposition – which increased the resistance to the change and worse, took the shape of a silent 'rebellion' in their minds. For all future matters, it was decided that a planned approach would be used to involve employees through focus groups, workshops, demonstrations and department/team meetings. This would make employees feel that they are part of the gradual change.

Last stage or the 'refreeze' stage entails adopting the new and changed state as the regular way of doing things. The change in premises brought a flux in employees' lives. They were not given any support, guidance or information as to how they were expected to cope with it. In the new location, employees took some time to adjust with the new surroundings, a new routine and new life style. This should have been accomplished by giving employees some time to adapt and then by providing positive reinforcement to continue the behaviour. Coaching, counselling and mentoring should have been provided in order to attain this. HR department should have been equipped enough to guide employees and to safeguard them of any subsidiary effects of these changes. This would have helped build trust in minds of employees towards the management that there was sufficient handholding for them to adjust with the changed situation.

Post the feedback of employees in the correction phase, such measures were implemented however, problems had already become severe by then.

SUCCESSION PLANNING

Temporary staffing had helped XY Associates to tide over some of the issues related to backlog of work. However, the Special Assignment Team suggested that succession planning was the key to ensuring a steady supply of talent in the future.

One of the problems faced by the organization was the un-preparedness of the junior recruiters to handle the complex and critical accounts. Lack of exposure and inability of these employees to tackle senior level recruitments was something due to which they were not able to contribute to the demands of business. Dependency on few resources to perform critical tasks harmed the work flow. This clearly indicated that succession planning was not something that the leaders or the human resources paid sufficient attention to.

Succession planning can be one of the most effective ways to build a stronger organization, to achieve the organizational goals and to prepare for unexpected events (Kapoor, 2015). With proper planning, XY Associates too could have managed to redeem itself from the crisis to some extent.

Special Assignment team along with the Human Resources department created an initial framework of the plan that outlined some action items.

Identification of its existing competencies and offerings to the market and industry was the first step. They analysed the kind of placement solutions they were proficient in, skills set the IT and ITES industries required etc., as those were the industries where in they primarily operated and had ample network in. Positions that had been closed for previous client assignments were analysed to find out the resources and skills needed for working on those positions. Requirement of competencies was documented.

Next step was mapping of these competencies with the available talent in the organization. Every recruiter was interviewed regarding the kind of assignments he or she had been successful with in the past. They were asked to fill up a questionnaire to assess themselves on various parameters. Feedback from respective supervisors was used as supporting source for this information. These responses were then collated to create an inventory of skills. This gave sufficient idea as to what kind of capability currently existed in the organization indicating thereby what needed to be developed and inculcated from within.

Long term training programs were then developed to cover the gap between existing and required skills. A professional with expertise in the field of training and development was hired so as to create and impart trainings for recruiters. This also helped to create a repository of training material that was used for every new recruiter at XY Associates in future. Coaching and mentoring juniors was added as a key responsibility area for all recruiters.

CONCLUSION

This entire episode was a learning experience for XY Associates which reminded the Management of the importance of manpower and drew their attention to various other significant problems in their functioning. All efforts were being made to mend the situation in the short and the long term. It had lost some of its most promising and loyal employees in the bargain to save cost and increase profitability. The result of all this was loss of clients, erosion of employee faith and total chaos. It was an awakening for the leadership and it realised the importance of communication as a very powerful tool to bind an organization with its employees and value of planning its actions effectively.

QUESTIONS FOR DISCUSSION

1. Do you think that the reaction of employees to the change proposed by the Management was justified? Explain.
2. What were the reasons due to which Management delayed communicating the change to employees? As a part of Management team, what would have been your approach to communicating this change?
3. Some issues that XY faced stemmed from the culture of the organization. Discuss.
4. Discuss any alternative or additional actions that the Special Assignment Team could have taken.
5. Devise a change management plan for the said change based on the Kurt Lewin change management model.

REFERENCES

Dessler, G. (2008). *Human Resource Management.* Prentice Hall, Inc.

Kapoor, S. (2015). *Human Resource Management (Text & Cases).* New Delhi: Taxmann Publications (P.) Ltd.

Kurt Lewin. (2016, January 28). Retrieved January 10, 2016, from Wikipedia: https://en.m.wikipedia.org/wiki/Kurt_Lewin

Lewin's Change Management Model. (2016, January 28). Retrieved January 10, 2016, from https://www.mindtools.com/pages/article/newPPM_94.htm

Shrivastava, S. (2014, November 28). *Change management: The HR perspective.* Retrieved January 10, 2016, from https://www.peoplematters.in/article/2014/11/28/culture/change-management-the-hr-perspective/7048

Singh, K. (2009). *Organizational Behaviour: Text and Cases.* New Delhi: Pearson Education.

The Kurt Lewin Change Management Model. (2016, January 28). Retrieved January 15, 2016, from http://www.change-management-coach.com/kurt_lewin.html

CHAPTER 17

Knowledge versus Power: Industrial Dispute in an Academic Institution

EXECUTIVE SUMMARY

Managing a healthy and engaging work environment has been a continuing challenge both for the academia and industry alike. Issues like industrial disputes and lack of harmony are frequently reported in cases of large corporations and industries but off-late these issues are on an alarming increase in academic institutions, which have been known as seats of learning and capability development centers for students and budding teaching professionals. This case portrays the instance of a self-financed state university affiliated academic institution from the Indian state of West Bengal where internal discords have started hindering the learning and academic process and have also put the jobs and careers of several students and teaching professionals in a state of uncertainty and insecurity.

Keywords: Industrial Disputes, Self-Financed Academic Institution, Political Unrest, Teacher Agitation, Employee Relations

INDRANIL MUTSUDDI

Indranil has more than 12 years of teaching experience in reputed B Schools across India. Presently he is working as Assistant Professor-HR in Amity Global Business School, Amity University, Noida. He has done PGDM (HRM), M.Sc. and had received certification for Entrepreneurship teaching from NEN & NSTEDB. He is pursuing PhD (Management) Amity University Noida. He had received Double Gold Medals from AIMA and Prof. Narendra Mohan Basu Award from Presidency College Kolkata. He had been the winner of Best Paper Awards at National Conferences. He had authored 3 books in HR that have been included in the syllabi of Universities like Bangalore University, JNTU Hyderabad, Solapur University, Shivaji University etc. He had authored 43 papers in various National/International journals, presented 27 papers in National/International Conferences and had contributed 5 chapters in edited executive books. His cases have been published in reputed management journals and text books in HRM.

SETTING THE STAGE

Gautam dragged himself into the room of Mr. Uttam Banerjee, President, of Sunshine Group of Institutions, Gopalpur. He knew well what the conversation would be about and how it would affect him personally and his family. Gautam was a faculty of Information Technology who had a vast experience in teaching and training in reputed cities like Pune, Mumbai and Hyderabad. The critical condition of his ailing father in Kolkata was perhaps one of the major issues why he had decided to relocate at Gopalpur. He had shifted to Gopalpur with family, after he had accepted the offer from Sunshine Institute of Management (SIM) a part of Sunshine Group of Institutions. The short distance between Gopalpur and Kolkata helped him to be with his parents during the weekends and look after his father. He hoped this move could facilitate his work-life balance.

Mr. Uttam Banerjee had sent for faculty members like Gautam and others to convey the decision of the management for being unable to continue with the payment of the compensation structure that they had been receiving in the past. In a soft, cold voice, he said, "Gautam, in the context of continued lack of admission and political unrest influencing the institution, we are going through a severe fund crunch. We have not been able to pay your regular salaries since January. We will be unable to continue with the present pay structure. We have taken a decision to freeze all the future admissions this year and complete the present academic batches of MBA and M.Sc(IT). We are offering you to give your resignation with immediate effect, so as to discontinue with your present pay structure. After your resignation and submission of a fresh application for joining this institution as a contractual faculty, Dr. Shome, the Director In-Charge, would be issuing you a fresh appointment letter with a new pay structure, which would be about 55% of your present salary. In the meantime if you are to get any offer from any other organization we will clear all your pending dues. However with the continuation of this contractual service, your dues might be cleared in phases. We solicit your cooperation." Gautam was rendered speechless. After the loss of his father last month, and almost 4 months of working without salary, he was already extremely dejected. Gautam came out of Mr. Banerjee's chamber. Other faculty members who were waiting outside Mr. Banerjee's chamber gauged Gautam's reaction.

ORGANIZATION BACKGROUND

It was a promising beginning when Mr. Banerjee had single handedly founded Sunshine Institute of Hotel and Catering Management in Gopalpur, one of the most promising industrial hubs in eastern India and West Bengal. As a dynamic young MBA graduate, Mr. Banerjee was determined to do something novel of his own. With a Government Regional Engineering College running very well and with the backdrop of a growing education industry, he thought it would be a golden opportunity to start a professional academic institution. There were also speculations of two more private engineering colleges being established. So he thought of starting a Hotel Management College. Initially the college was started in a two storied rented apartment located in Town Plaza, the heart of the town, Gopalpur. With rented premises, it was difficult to get an affiliation from the only state technical university. Mr. Banerjee had to get a full-fledged campus – to satisfy the regulatory requirements. One of his friends suggested him to apply for land for his college to the authorities. The required land was acquired with the help of his friend Karabi, the daughter of a reputed politician who later went on be his wife. Sunshine Institute of Hotel and Catering Management was launched. Uttam was ambitious and he wanted Sunshine Group of Institutions to be at its best in the region.

The "Sunshine Educational Trust", a non-profit educational society, was established by Mr. Uttam with the support from some notable industrialists and political figures of Gopalpur. The trust had a sole objective to promote professional education and skill development in the region. The inauguration of the society was done in a grand function. The incorporation of the Sunshine Group of Institutions was also announced at the same event. The event was covered extensively by the media. Mr. Uttam made headlines in all local news as a budding edupreneur (education entrepreneur).

Sunshine Group initially started with under graduate Programs in Hotel and Tourism Management. With an excellent campus and infrastructure, strong recommendation of the industrial community and political support the institute got affiliations for the programs from the State's University of Technology. Within few months of its inception, with a team of capable and experienced faculty members, the institute earned a reputation of being one of the leading Hotel Management colleges in eastern India. It was smooth sailing in the beginning as the institute had a steady inflow of students joining various courses during the commencement of the new academic session.

THE VALUES, BELIEFS AND INTELLECTUAL CAPITAL OF SUNSHINE

The institute started with an objective of providing quality management education, nurturing professional skills at the highest level and imbibing holistic development of young minds so as to develop managers and leaders of the future.

The institute had believed in the values of imparting holistic growth of students and its faculty team had worked very well to establish its brand name in Eastern India and the corporate world. The management had always encouraged the belief of ensuring highest standards of teaching as the prime hallmark of the institution. For achieving its business objective the institute had hired the best intellectual capital in the team of its faculty members comprising of professionals from the hotel and tourism industry as well as experienced academicians from reputed institutions. Although the institute had started with a meagre strength of 10 faculties, with the inception of another campus, the total strength grew to 90 teaching staffs, 20 administrative staffs and 40 utility/support staff.

Figure 1: Organizational Structure of Sunshine Group of Institutions

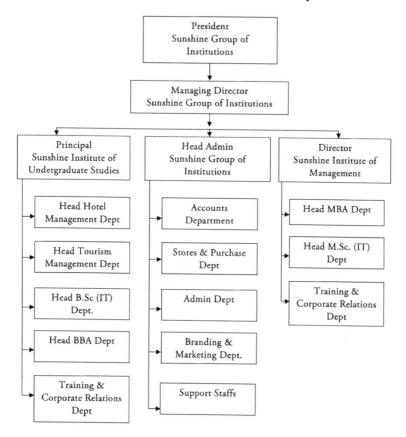

CLOUDS IN THE SKY: ADVENT OF THE CRISIS

The Human Resources team was not headed by a professional and experienced person. The person heading the department was a close affiliate of the Banerjee family. Faculty recruitments were made on the basis of the recommendations prescribed by the heads of the academic departments. The team did not have concrete HR plan or budget to streamline the recruitment process. Staff files and personal records were hardly given proper attention. Although the accounts team ensured stringent documentation of clearing statutory requirements like provident fund deduction, professional tax deduction and income tax deduction, the HR team was lacking in putting up serious professional effort to bring up a strong HR system for managing the human resource related affairs of the institution. Most of the HR decisions were passed on to the top management under the discretion of Mrs. Banerjee who was the highest signing authority regarding all HR decisions in the organization.

Most of the time, the institute was overspending on its branding and marketing activities. Huge colour advertisements were put on leading Bengali, English and Hindi newspapers. Large hoardings advertising the various courses were put on major cities. Large sum of money was spent on signing Memorandum of Understanding (MOU) with local student recruitment agents in the adjoining states like Bihar and Jharkhand without having any feasibility analysis done.

THE EXPANSION DECISION

It was March 2010, the management of Sunshine Group of institutions decided to apply to the affiliating University for increasing the number of seats for all the programs run by the institute. In the first phase the institute hired 25 additional faculty members in lecturer positions, mostly fresh pass-out for its Under Graduate wing. The University inspection went off very well during the end of June 2010 and the college got the nod for admitting 120 students for its MBA and M.Sc (IT) programs.

Mr. Banerjee instructed Mr. Tapan, Head Branding & Marketing department to start a rigorous marketing drive to ensure student admission for the newly allotted seats. It is worth mentioning that it had been hardly a month that Mr. Tapan and Ms. Sutapa were hired to head and lead the Marketing department (previously known as Admissions Departments) of the group with a lucrative pay package from a rival institute.

THE FIRST TREMOR

The results of seat allotment after the completion of Common Entrance Test (CET) organized by the University were shocking. Hardly 63 students had opted for MBA and 40 students had opted for M.Sc (IT) programs. On the other hand students opting for Undergraduate programs were marginally better as compared to the previous year.

Faculty members who had represented the institute during the counseling sessions organized by the University observed that most parents were eager to admit their wards in Kolkata or outside Bengal particularly in Bangalore and Pune citing drastic fall in new job opportunities in Eastern India and Bengal. For the first time in the history of Sunshine Group of Institutions, during the month of September there was a fund crunch and the salary disbursement for the month of August was delayed by two weeks. It was beginning of the downfall.

Later on during the month of October the management spent lavishly for its first ever Management & IT conference, soon followed by the "Bijoya Dashami feast". The institute went on spending heavily on activities that were perhaps unnecessary in the context of the current situation. There was poor placement, first time in the history of the institution. This was further worsened by poor selection of students for summer internship projects in reputed companies. The management remained adamant on scaling up their growing investments on advertisements in leading newspapers on a regular basis.

There were growing incidences of lack of agreement between the junior faculty members belonging to the Sunshine Institute of Under Graduate Studies and the senior faculty members, including the Head of the department regarding allotment of lectures, duties and involvement of faculty members in various supporting administrative activities. Many of them had worked more than eight months without the receipt of any formal appointment letter from the management. They even tried to reach Mrs. Banerjee, MD of the Sunshine Group and each time the HR Head had somehow prevented them to interact with the higher authorities on issues related to employment terms and conditions. On the other hand the senior faculty members were also dissatisfied with the issue of their own pay packages offered by the institution.

The admin department soon had to mitigate two looming issues – the first being the demand for implementing 6th pay commission salary package demanded by the senior faculty members and the growing unrest among the junior faculty members. A few days later in March 2011, the junior members too joined hands along with the senior faculty members demanding 6th pay commission salary structure in their pay. On the other hand with poor admissions last academic session and excess faculty recruitment in anticipation of higher student admission the management was already going through a crunched financial situation. Initially all the demands were rejected stating the poor state of admissions in the college.

Admission process was over for June 2011. Yet the picture was hardly rosy for Sunshine. A delegation of faculty members constituting senior and junior faculty members met Mr. Uttam demanding revision of their pay structure and implementation of the 6th pay commission salary in the institute. The management took a decision to revise the pay package of the senior faculty members and program heads. They commented that the package of the junior faculties would be reviewed only after the annual appraisal on completion of their probation period in the institute.

THE STORM

The outrage among the junior faculty members at Sunshine Institute of Undergraduate Studies took its first shape when there was an outright argument between one of the junior faculty members and Prof. Subhomoy Dey, Principal of Sunshine Institute of Undergraduate Studies. The faculty was issued show cause letter. In reply, the faculty alleged that Prof. Dey had been continuously harassing and torturing her without any valid reason. The issue took a serious shape when a large chunk of junior faculties decided to join the State University Teacher's Association of Gopalpur. The Sunshine chapter of the Association was ceremoniously inaugurated in the common room with the management boycotting the event. The management decided to remain silent on the issue and adopted a wait and watch approach in order to evaluate actions taken by the association. The association invited other teaching and non-teaching staff to support them by saying that the objective of this association was primarily to help the institute achieve its academic excellence which they believed had fallen apart during the last one year.

Within one and half week of its inception, beyond the expectation of the management and other staffs, the governing body of the association submitted a one page charter of demands to the management. They requested the management:

1. To review the show cause order of their colleague who was now an active member of the association
2. To persuade the Principal of Sunshine Institute of Undergraduate Studies to improve his exploitative approach towards junior faculty members

3. To issue appointment letters for all junior faculty members with the implementation of the 6th pay commission pay scale.

Mr. Uttam Banerjee was furious with the sheet of charter of demands placed by the association. He fumed, "This is an academic institution! How can you people allow these people to start an association? The junior faculty members have hardly any experience, they would have to complete their probation, go through the annual appraisal process and if we find them eligible for continuance of service then review of pay scale could be thought off."

Mr. Banerjee's opinion on the issue was duly forwarded to the association members. By the time the management asked the principal of Sunshine Institute of Undergraduate Studies and Director of Sunshine Institute of Management to immediately start the annual performance review process. This action infuriated the members of the association. They warned all the existing and new faculty members from participating in the annual appraisal process. They declared that the appraisal was not legitimate as they all were selected in presence and approval of the members of the faculty recruitment committee of the state university to which the institution was affiliated. There was chaos in both the campuses. The association members decided to go for a pen down day and hold a peaceful demonstration at the college gate. An unpleasant incident occurred with the arrival of Mr. Uttam's car at the college gate. The association members blocked the entrance and prevented the car from entering the college premises. When Mr. Uttam Banerjee de-boarded his car, he was immediately surrounded by the agitating members of the union. The disaster started with a vocal argument between Mr. Hirak Chakraborty, the General Secretary of the Association and Mr. Banerjee. The senior faculty members and other staffs from inside the college rushed to the rescue of Mr. Banerjee. He claimed that Mr. Chakraborty had physically assaulted him. The college authorities went for an immediate suspension of classes and shut the main entrance of the college.

Media rushed to the college and police had to intervene and disperse the huge crowd which had gathered at the institute gate. The management declared a two day shut down in order to settle the issue. The association claimed that the management had asked the police to indiscriminately physically assault their peaceful gathering.

On the second day, the representatives of the management, members of the association and the police sat together to sort out the issues. The association demanded that the management would have to apologize and compensate for assault incident, which was rejected on the spot. They said that the institute would not compromise with the association members who had violated the very dignity of teachers by behaving like rogues. With hardly any resolution in the meeting, the management issued a show cause to Mr. Chakraborty, the General Secretary of the Association and other members for their unruly behaviour. Upon non-receipt of any reply from the Association, the management decided to sack all the 32 members of the association including Mr. Hirak Chakraborty with immediate effect.

TWIST IN THE TALE

The course of events took an unexpected twist when it was found that Mr. Hirak Chakraborty was the son of a local political leader of the new ruling party in Bengal. The local party wing declared that Hirak was a leader of their "Siksha-Cell" (Education Wing) and his suspension was an insult to their party. The next day hundreds of party activists gathered at the gate of Sunshine Institute of Undergraduate Studies with party flags, posters and festoons demanding the downfall of the management. The party activists thronged in huge numbers and locked the main gate of the institution preventing employees and management representatives entering the college premises. Mr. Chakraborty and his association members decided to sit for an indefinite fast protesting the exploitation and humiliation. Classes were suspended for several days. Students suffered and the parents were infuriated by the rigid stand of the management and the association members.

Although the political unrest was later defused, Mr. Hirak and his associates lodged a case against the management stating the decisions taken by the management were inhumane. The political unrest around the institution had far reaching consequences. The classes remained suspended and students joined the agitation along with their parents. A gross misconduct of academic activities was reported to the University. After a survey of the situation, the University found the situation beyond control. They informed the college authorities that they were going to withdraw the affiliation for all courses run by the institute for the forthcoming academic session. Admission for the new academic session was frozen in the light of the new information from the university. The current students performed poorly in the end term exams and their placements were dismal. Many faculty members decided to quit in search of greener pastures with their salaries being withheld by the management due to lack of funds. Loyal faculty members and staff who were still attached with the institute with the hope of a better day were left severely disappointed with long unpaid months of service.

Sunshine Group of Institutions was once again in the headlines for the phenomenal teacher agitation and the political turmoil around the institution. With all the roadblocks looming large, the management decided to discontinue any further classes leading to the shutdown of the institution.

CHALLENGES FACING THE ORGANIZATION

The management of Sunshine failed to foresee the storm brewing in its sky. Being rigid in its approach led the organization to its imminent downfall. Apart from its inherent weakness in harnessing a professional HR approach in terms of managing people the management hardly had any proactive strategy to counter conflicts before they had swept the organization to its imminent end. Having inexperience professionals in important positions was another contributing factor. For running a professional institution it was a strategic need for Sunshine to have experienced professionals leading the institution. People who seemed to be helpful had actually corroded interpersonal relationships and employee relations that led to the disaster. There was hardly any contingency plan to pacify the growing dissent among the junior teachers. Issues like respect, concern for interpersonal relationships, trust were ignored at the bottom level that infused a climate of distrust, hatred and conflict among people.

THE WAY FORWARD

With the situation gradually slipping out of control the management had no option but to stop the functioning of the institute. Admissions were frozen as the institution did not receive continuation of the University affiliation due to gross misconduct of academic activities. Faculty and staff left the organization looking for greener pastures. With no options available, the management decided to announce a formal shut down of the institution.

QUESTIONS FOR DISCUSSION

1. What went wrong with Sunshine Group of Institutions?
2. Do you think that this organization had a proper HR intervention to deal with the case? Justify your answer.
3. Explain the industrial conflict issues discussed in the case.
4. What would have been your suggestions to the management of Sunshine Group of Institutions from a HR perspective?

CHAPTER 18

From Losers to Winners: A Case Study on Effective Leadership

EXECUTIVE SUMMARY

The case talks about a team called "Cheetay" from Zuby India Pvt. Ltd. The team was constantly failing to deliver and was the most under-performing teams in the NEZ (North East Zone) Circle of Zuby India Pvt. Ltd. Management was concerned as the team handled one of the biggest markets of the company. After trying many things the management decided to replace the team leader. As soon as the Team Leader was replaced, the team showed a complete turnaround and reached the top position within a month. The case focuses on changes in team performance with a change in leaders and their leadership style, provided that other factors remained unchanged. This case discusses how a leader with his participative leadership style took his team from a low performer status to a top performer status of the organisation. The factors which led to this shift in the team performance were – trust, recognition, motivation, participation, empathy and constant guidance by the leader. People skills and Emotional Quotient were essential to develop a cordial relationship between team members and their Leader. Leaders possessing these skills always get the support from their team-members and receive their enthusiastic participation no matter how challenging the situations are.

Keywords: Leadership, Effective Leadership Style, Communication, Trust, Motivation, Team Performance, Emotional Quotient.

AMOD PRAKASH SINGH

Amod has worked as Management Trainee - Sales for Hawkins Cookers Ltd., looking after Industrial, CSD, Modern Retail and Civil sales in Pune and South Maharashtra Territory. He has also worked as RM- Prepaid Distribution at Vodafone in UP-East Circle.

An MBA (Marketing & ITM) from KIIT School of Management, KIIT University – Bhubaneswar, he has studied SAP-ERP under SAP University Alliance Program and has working knowledge of SD, MM, PP Modules on Sandbox Server. He is a BSc. graduate from St. Andrew's College. He was awarded Merit Recognition Certificate for scoring 97 percentile in 4th National IT Aptitude Test. He has participated in "SAP's National Dashboard Designing Competition".

Previous Publications:

1. A study of Bharti Airtel Limited and Bihar Telecom Circle.
    Journal : Arth Prabhand: A Journal of Economics and Management.
    Vol.2, Issue 4 April 2013; ISSN 2278-0629

2. Mind and market share of Bharti Airtel Ltd. in Bihar telecom circle. Journal : Asia Pacific Journal of Research in Business Management. Volume 4, Issue 4 (April, 2013); ISSN 2229-4104

PRIYA SAMANT

Priya has worked as a visiting faculty in Amity University. She worked as an Assistant Professor at Beehive College of Management and Technology, Dehradun. She has worked as a Lecturer for about two years at Dass College of Management and Technology, Dehradun. She also has sales experience as sales representative at Masicon Financial Ltd, Dehradun.

Priya completed her Master's Degree in Business Administration from Institute of Management Studies, Dehradun in 2009. She holds Bachelor's degree in Science from DAV (PG) College, Dehradun in the year 2007. She published and presented a research paper titled "Digitalization of Rural Communities: Problems and Remedies" at International an conference. She has also published paper abstract titled "Role of ICTs in empowering rural women".

SETTING THE STAGE

Mr. Sachin Kumar sat worried in his cabin. He had just finished a video conference with his Circle Management Team and felt stressed by the aftermath. His Team was constantly failing to achieve their targets, missing deadlines and seemed unaligned. Members were de-motivated and their performance had hit rock bottom. Most of the members were waiting for the annual appraisals in order to switch for better opportunities. The team was ranked last amongst 10 teams and maintained the same position months after months. There seemed to be no change in team's performance even after consistent support and motivation by the Circle Management. It was then decided by the Management that it was time for some remedial action; after careful deliberation it was decided that the Team Leader should be changed. It was also decided that all other conditions as team members, territory structure, etc will be unchanged. The under-performing team suddenly fired up and reached the top spot within no time. Not only did it achieve the 1st rank but maintained the position for several months. The team members seemed highly motivated and satisfied. There seemed a new energy in them. What had suddenly happened to the team?

ORGANIZATION BACKGROUND

Zuby India Pvt. Ltd. (ZIPL) was one of the largest Telecom Companies in India as per its subscriber base, after Talkmore. It had its headquarters in Mumbai and had nearly 184 million subscribers as of April 2015. Zuby India Pvt. Ltd. was a 100% owned subsidiary of Zuby Group, Portugal. It commenced operations in 1994 when Peterson Telecom (which was later bought by Zuby Plc.) bought the mobile service license for Mumbai Circle. Zuby Brand was formally launched in India in September 2007, when Zuby Plc. purchased the majority stake in Peterson Telecom in May 2007. From a single telecom operator having 3.1 million customers, the company had grown its operations to cover all the 20 telecom circles of India and having a combined subscriber base of nearly 184 million subscribers. This depicted the commitment and success of Zuby India Pvt. Ltd. in a highly competitive and price sensitive Indian Telecom Market. It had its operations in prepaid as well as post-paid cellular telecom segments, with excellent coverage throughout India. Zuby India Pvt. Ltd. added maximum customers in July 2014 when 13.6 million new customers joined its network in that month.

In May 2010, Zuby India Pvt. Ltd. paid INR 1161.78 million for purchasing telecom spectrum in 9 circles. The circles in which it provided 3G services were - Delhi, Gujarat, Haryana, Kolkata, Maharashtra & Goa, Mumbai, Tamil Nadu, Uttar Pradesh (East) and West Bengal.

Zuby India Pvt. Ltd. sold its services through an extensive network of more than 2 hundred thousand retailers spread across the country. The company had its presence in Metro cities, semi-urban, rural and even in the deep rural interiors of the country.

INTRODUCTION

Zuby India Pvt. Ltd. was one of the largest Telecom Companies in India. It had its operations distributed across all the 20 circles in the country. These circles were further divided into smaller Zones within each Circle, for better operational ease. These Zones were further divided into smaller Branches based on ease of operation feasibility.

Figure 1: Organisational structure of Zuby India Ltd.

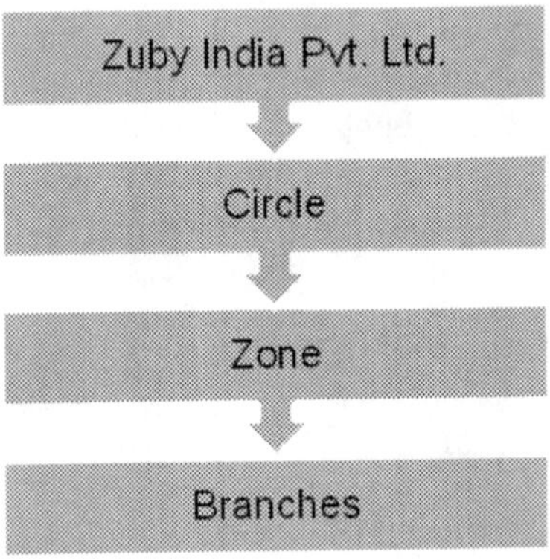

NEZ circle was one of its largest circles with respect to customer base as well as revenue. NEZ circle was divided into 6 different Zones with 10 Branches in all. Each branch had a Distribution team. The team members were responsible for managing the business in the branch. The business was divided amongst them on the basis of individual's territory. An Individual's Territory comprised of distributors channel and their respective market. They were responsible for Sales and Channel Management. They had to manage Sales of Prepaid / Post-paid Connections, D-Rupia (mobile banking product), Distribution Channel, Distributors Audit, Networks Operation, etc. in their assigned territory.

To increase competition among the teams, the teams were ranked on various operational parameters. Each Team member was ranked as per their performance compared to other team members at the same level, throughout the circle. As a sum of the performance of team members, the Branch was ranked amongst all other Branches. Further as the sum of performance of Branch or Branches the Zone was ranked amongst all Zones of the Circle.

"Cheetey" was one of the 10 Branches in NEZ Circle. It was headed by Mr. Kumar who was a hard task master and the employees were not at ease with him.

Figure 2: Team structure of Zuby India Pvt. Ltd

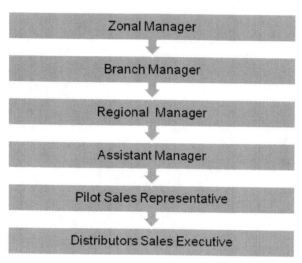

Zonal Manager

↓

Branch Manager

↓

Regional Manager

↓

Assistant Manager

↓

Pilot Sales Representative

↓

Distributors Sales Executive

THE CASE

Employees were greeted at 9.15am by Mr. Kumar, through a conference call connecting all the 4 Regional Managers and 18 Assistant Managers of the branch. In this morning call, circle targets and agenda of the day were discussed, the Branch agenda was briefed to the team members and individual team agenda were discussed alongside.

Purpose of the call was also to review the previous day's targets and team achievements. Explanations were sought for not achieving commitments. Tempers ran high; team members were humiliated in public. They were asked to add their previous lag to the day's commitment and then achieve an escalated target. The reasons for under achievement of targets were evident. The Regional Managers could not empathize with the Assistant Managers, as they knew Mr. Kumar will not accept any non-conformity of his instructions. Assistant Managers and Executives were not given any authority to take any decisions and everything needed Mr. Kumar's approval. Any achievement by the team was show-cased by Mr. Kumar as his personal accomplishment but he never took responsibility of any failures. He sometimes communicated to the Assistant Managers without the knowledge of Regional Managers. This created confusion and mistrust in the chain of command and as a result mutual trust was missing within the team.

DURING THE DAY

Through the day, Mr. Kumar repeatedly made calls to the Assistant Managers along with their respective Regional Managers to discuss the current achievement status of the day's agenda. This resulted in a sense of panic and stress in the team. No one was happy or content with their work. Mr. Kumar's formidable demeanour discouraged the staff to express themselves. As the team was lagging on all fronts so they were made to work late in the evenings and on week-ends to cope with the targets.

During the course of the day, members of the team were called several times to enquire about the progress of their assigned tasks, this caused a hindrance in their working. They lost interest as same things were repeatedly enquired time and again during the day. This also left them with less time to focus on the current agenda. Hence the overall productivity of the team reduced drastically.

END OF THE DAY

Despite repeated discussions during the day, in the evening too the whole team was connected through a conference call. The team members were asked to state their achievements as per the commitments made in the morning. The team members failing on some or the other front were reprimanded in front of the whole team including seniors and subordinates. This created a feeling of frustration and mistrust amongst the team members. They were discontented with this work culture but did not know whom to approach with their problems.

Fig 3: Team structure of "Cheetey" branch

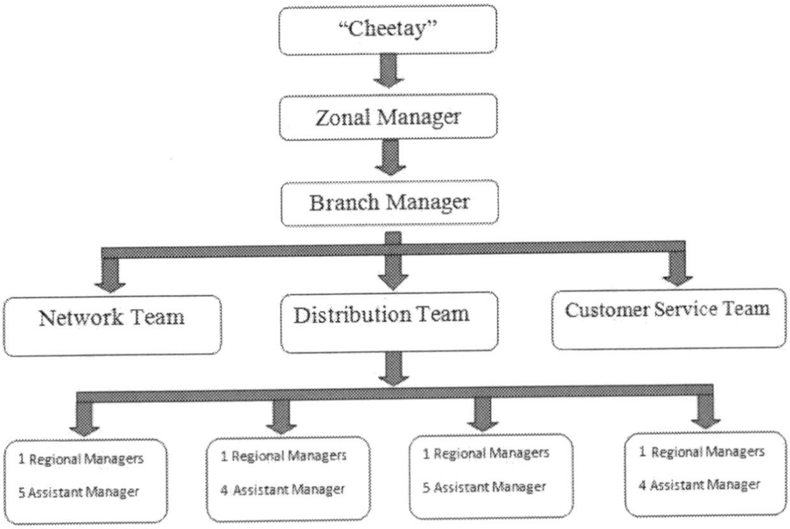

The team members were discouraged to take autonomous decisions and were asked to strictly follow what was instructed and not to deviate from Mr. Kumar's agenda. They were losing their self-confidence with each passing day.

Team members were threatened with pink slips in case of under-achievement. The individuals were blamed continuously and no effort was undertaken to solve the problem collectively as a team. The situation was deteriorating continuously. Employees were de-motivated, management was clueless and no one had belief on either himself or his team.

The Circle Leadership Team was worried about working of NEZ Circle. In September (2011), the Circle Leadership Team took a decision to replace Mr. Kumar. Hence Mr. Suresh Kapoor joined Cheetey as their Manager from October (2011). He was earlier leading the "Fasaadi" team - another team of NEZ Circle, which was ranked 1st amongst the teams.

THE WAY FORWARD

One of the first steps taken by Mr. Kapoor was building the lost confidence of the team members. He took meetings with each Assistant Manager, along with his team members so as to understand their problems. He treated each team as a separate entity because problems and solutions were different for each team. He patiently listened to each team member and his individual perspective. Their queries were heard. He discussed the solutions with the teams and encouraged them to decide the best solutions themselves. He made them realize their value in the organization in terms of the revenue they generated for the organization and the business they handled which in turn added value to the organization. The tasks were set by the teams themselves keeping in mind the monthly targets. The teams were encouraged to drive at one major agenda per day so as to give it undivided attention. The members were motivated to perform better. They were being given full autonomy and support while working in their Territories. Mr. Kapoor was ready to help each team whenever required. He treated everyone with due respect and took Assistant Managers in confidence before talking to any member of his team, this resulted in an increased trust and bonding between the team members.

The teams were provided with flexible working hours. Team members and Assistant Managers were warned against compelling anyone to work beyond the working hours. No call policy was implemented after working hours and on weekly-offs. On Saturdays he started organising teams get together. Family get-togethers were also arranged. Teams were involved in group celebrations of different festivals. "Rewards and Recognition Programme" was implemented to increase their motivation level. Mr. Kapoor was successful in winning the confidence of the team members.

These efforts resulted in better team functioning and the performance of Cheetey miraculously improved. A team which consistently under-performed, achieved the top rank and sustained its position for several months. They were focused on winning and staying ahead.

QUESTIONS FOR DISCUSSION

Q1. According to the case what do you think were the determinants for under performance of the team "Cheetay"?

Q2. What do you think were the strategies implemented by the management of Zuby India Pvt. Ltd. before changing the team leader?

Q3. Do you consider Mr. Kumar a true leader? Give reasons to support your answer.

Q4. Discuss how Mr. Suresh Kapoor completely turned the situation of team 'Cheetey'.

Q5. Had the management not changed the team leader what could have been the options for Zuby India Pvt. Ltd.?

CHAPTER 19

Faculty Attrition in World Class Skill Centre: A Way through the Labyrinth

EXECUTIVE SUMMARY

Success of any organisation depends on its human capital who strives hard to achieve the organisational goals. If the human resource of an organisation is properly motivated, it will ensure long term survival of the organisation. It also becomes imperative for an organisation to enhance job engagement, motivation and to ensure that the staff are rewarded and valued for what they achieve and do. This study presents the case of World Class Skill Centre (WCSC) at Vivek Vihar, New Delhi which had failed to recognise the potential of non-financial motivation of its Master Trainers and had resultantly faced increased faculty attrition. Although everything was in place as far as policies were concerned but the trainers were overburdened with work, unscrupulous work culture and supervisory pressures. Master Trainers were asked to perform clerical work of handling ancillary departments like stores, laundry etc. and were not given teaching roles for which they were hired and trained for. World Class Skill Centre had failed to implement the innovative policies and practices that were put in place for the growth of the trainers and ultimately the organisation. This case has been formulated to understand the effect of attrition on an organisation. It will also discuss the importance of non-monetary motivation for enhancing the morale of the employees and simultaneously decreasing their attrition rate.

Keywords: Faculty attrition, Retention, Employee engagement, Employee assessment, Motivation.

VIKAS GUPTA

Vikas is an alumnus of Institute of Hotel Management, Gwalior, Madhya Pradesh and holds Master's degree in Tourism Management and Bachelor degree in Hospitality and Hotel Administration. He also holds a Diploma in Training and Development from Indian Society for Training and Development. Apart from his academic credentials he possesses exemplary leadership and training skills, making him a really sought after professional especially in the fields of Food Production and Culinary Arts. He has rich and extensive experience of teaching for more than seven years in both India and abroad with renowned names such as Café Coffee Day, Fiji National University, Amity University and Various Central and State IHM's in India. He is presently working with Amity University, Noida, Uttar Pradesh as an Assistant Professor in the field of Hospitality. He also has a very good research background with publications in National and International Journals and Conference Proceedings.

SETTING THE STAGE

Adil Ahmed, a Master trainer at World Class Skill Centre (WCSC) was sincere, hard-working and a God fearing man. His otherwise smooth routine life was now in a mess and additionally he was not keeping well. Adil sat outside the doctor's cabin, thinking what could be the reason of his throbbing headaches which had become more frequent of late. The doctor called Adil inside his cabin and told him that the reports had come in and the headaches were a result of hypertension. He was advised to take it easy with his work, take some rest, and avoid any kind of tension. It was going to be hard; the excessive pressure at WCSC was taking a toll on his health. He had been thinking of quitting for quite some time now – "This is it, I need to quit!" he said to himself.

World Class Skill Centre (WCSC) had been formed with an aim to recruit highly qualified and skilled Master Trainers who would ensure that the organisational aspirations are translated into effective and sustained action plan of skilling required workforce for a fast developing India. Mr. Adil although had been provided with competitive remuneration and all the necessary facilities was not keen to continue working with the organisation due to the ever increasing work pressure. The organisation seemed to lack commitment, drive and enthusiasm in its work force. The resignations of other Master Trainers kept piling up as the working culture remained un-progressive and no efforts were taken by management to bring down the churn rate. Resignation of Master Trainers was an accumulated effect of low employee morale, overloaded academic and non-academic schedules, and insipid employee relationships.

INTRODUCTION

Every country, whether it is developed or developing, requires a good vocational training system for the development of its industries and other sectors of income generation. It is very important to have a well-structured education system through which quality skill and knowledge can be instilled into the students who further contribute to the growth of the country. As per the Annual World Bank Report on Service Sectors of India (2014), India is one of the countries in the world where the working population in the urban areas is more than the people dependent on them and this trend is bound to continue for at least the next three decades. In recognition of this need, Government of India has planned to give national priority to skill development for the next ten years. The priority of the Government is not only to educate the workforce at top levels by providing refresher courses but also to provide skill training to lesser educated labour force. Figure 1 shows the skill pyramid to show the approach of Government of India for skill development.

Figure 1: Skill Pyramid

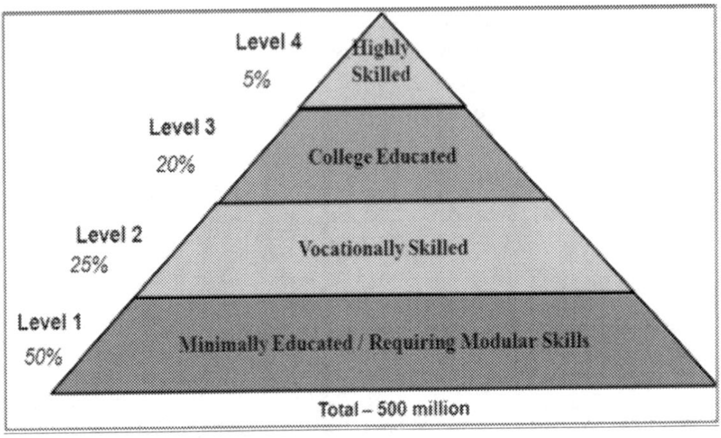

Source: IMaCS analysis, 2010.

For formulation of a strategy on skill development, a cabinet committee with representation from different ministries and National Skill Development Agency (NSDA) had been constituted. NSDA has been given a key role for coordinating the skill development programme in India. Thirty Eight Sector Skill Councils had been approved in Agriculture, Services, Manufacturing and Informal Sectors; and were given the responsibility to run certification, accreditation and "train the trainer" programmes in order to standardise the occupational standards. Funds have been allocated to setup new skill development centres in different parts of India where skill development programmes can be conducted and the work force can be trained.

To address the issue of shortage of skilled manpower in the sectors of Hospitality, Retail, Finance and Merchandising, the Government of India ordered the setting up of "World Class Skill Centre (WCSC)" in Delhi in collaboration with an international partner. Master Trainers had been recruited to provide skill based training to students who will become skilled manpower for future India.

Every organization recruits employees, acquiring their services, motivating them to raise their level of performance, developing their skills and ensuring that they maintain their commitment to the organization; these are the factors essential for achieving organizational objectives. Undoubtedly, success of an organisation depends on how it uses its resources especially human resources. In World Class Skill Centre, although all measures were taken to adequately utilise the human resources but the organisation incurred huge losses due to the increased attrition rate of its employees and this was due to certain unexpected factors which were not accounted for while formulating the policies of WCSC. Master Trainers such as Adil Ahmed felt that their job was not steady, there was very little career growth and promotional opportunities and the future looked bleak.

BACKGROUND OF THE CASE

World Class Skill Centre in New Delhi had been setup on the guidelines of National Skill Development Mission of Government of India to provide skill based training to more than 10000 students in a year in different fields. The setting up of World Class Skill Centre was a benchmark for other institutions offering vocational training in the country and had been conceived as a ground breaking effort of national interest. Government of India signed a Memorandum of Understanding (MOU) with the Government of Singapore to collaborate on this skill development project of national importance.

For providing effective skill training, "Master Trainers" had been hired in the relevant fields. They were competent and had been provided with all the necessary facilities at work. They had also been provided with adequate freedom of work and remuneration which was competitive with the industry standards. Yet due to some unknown reasons the employee attrition rate in WCSC grew steadily.

A high rate of employee attrition had put an increased burden on the organisation due to repeated process of recruitment, selection, and training. The costs incurred due to high attrition were direct and indirect costs. There was loss of expertise, low employee morale among the other trainers and loss of brand value of the organisation. The indirect cost components of attrition also included replacement costs, cost on employment advertisements to recruit new Master Trainers, entrance interviews, administrative functions, pre-employment and post-employment acquisitions. There were also costs incurred due to training, orientation of new recruits and of lost productivity due to the transition phase.

GOVERNMENT OF INDIA INITIATIVES FOR SKILL DEVELOPMENT IN INDIA

Government of India launched "Skill India" initiative in the year-2015 and under the aegis of this initiative various programmes like "Pradhan Mantri Kaushal Vikas Yojaya", and "National Skill Development Mission" were launched. These programmes were launched to provide skill based training at Central and State levels. Memorandums of Understanding (MOU's) were signed with different countries to provide skill training to Indian Citizens at par with international standards. Government of India also launched a website to provide education loans for the students under the "Skill Loan Scheme". This scheme has been formulated to provide education loans between INR 5000 to INR 1,50,000; to 3.4 million students who intend to develop their skills in the next 5 years (IBEF, 2016).

WORLD CLASS SKILL CENTRE (WCSC)

As an initiative of National Skill Development Mission (NSDM), the first World Class Skill Centre was commissioned at Vivek Vihar, New Delhi. It has been built to provide technical skills and knowledge to school pass outs and adult learners for further learning and employability. It has been designed to offer skill courses ranging from the streams of hospitality & tourism to biotechnology, merchandising, retail, nursing, IT and IT-enabled services, beauty and business studies. At WCSC, it was believed that quality training was its key to success. WCSC had also created a competitive advantage over the other institutions offering similar programmes through innovation & research, above par skill based training and use of latest technology.

To train the students in the fields of Hospitality, Finance, Merchandising and Retail a new post of "Master Trainers" was created to recruit a pool of talented professional who have hands-on experience in the relevant field and can train the students to become skilled manpower Mr. Adil Ahmed was one of them. The Master Trainers had been recruited keeping in mind their level of skills with regards to their area of specialisation. The recruitment had been done in a fair manner, with the help of a panel of academicians, industry professionals, and Institute of Technical Education (ITE) representatives through "walk-in" interviews.

ROLE OF INSTITUTE OF TECHNICAL EDUCATION (ITE), SINGAPORE IN DEVELOPING WCSC

The role of Institute of Technical Education (ITE), Singapore was to provide WCSC campus architectural plans and building infrastructure. It also provided advice on procurement of training equipment and commissioning of workshops. ITE conducted 'Train the Trainers' programmes apart from training of centre management staff. It also conducted inspections and evaluation of centre performance. The approach of WCSC was institution building rather than infrastructure creation; they intended to create skilled professionals who are valuable assets for the country.

Master Trainers were provided extensive and vigorous training of one month at ITE, Singapore as the training facilities offered were better than the facilities present in India. This training helped the Master Trainers to gain practical knowledge and provide quality skill based training to the students in consonance with international industry standards. The next five month training was provided in India and during this period of training they conceptualized the skills learnt in Singapore and applied them in WCSC. A total of INR 3 hundred thousand was allocated per Master Trainer to provide them training in Singapore which included the return air fare Delhi-Singapore-Delhi, daily allowances, hotel accommodation and food during their stay. Resultantly it became imperative for WCSC to retain these professionals for a longer term as the training costs were very high.

RETENTION POLICY

To retain the Master Trainers and motivate them, the remuneration offered to the trainers was at par with the industry standards. They were provided with ample opportunities so that they could also improve their skills in the relevant field as they progress with the organisation by conducting regular workshops and seminars on Skill development. It was mandatory for all Master Trainers to arrange for consultancies and submit the report to the Director of WCSC on a quarterly basis. The focus of WCSC during employee recruitment was to make sure that right people were hired and they should feel satisfied with their work and be associated with the organisation for a longer time period.

Focus of WCSC was on increasing the job understanding among the trainers and improvement measures for their performance. WCSC had taken adequate measure for taking care of its staff and developing their professional competence during their entire tenure at the organisation. Various formal and informal activities were also conducted to facilitate an environment of openness and friendliness among employees.

EMPLOYEE ASSESSMENT MEASURES AT WCSC

In WCSC, Employee assessment was done through pre-defined performance appraisal mechanism. Performance Appraisal System helped the management in judging the productivity and effectiveness of Master Trainers in their relevant areas. It included both the qualitative and quantitative parameters of the job performance of a trainer. It evaluated a trainer comprehensively through a set procedure including his or her performance of job and potential for development. It was a continuous procedure and its functional responsibility lay with the supervisor. The supervisor of all Master Trainers was the Director of WCSC. He allocated duties and prepared rosters for their training schedule on a weekly basis. He made sure that the work was done in its place and time, and also kept a check on how employees were performing their tasks on the basis of the assessment sheet.

The performance appraisal systems in place at WCSC were formally communicated to all Master Trainers. They were well aware of the performance parameters and were also convinced with the system in place. The process was long and took about three weeks to complete. The appraisal of the employees was based on their performance of the tasks assigned to them.

ATTRITION RATE OF MASTER TRAINERS IN WCSC

Sudden meetings were organised by the supervisor when Master Trainers started to leave for the day from their offices and the meetings went on for 2-3 hours. They were not given any kind of incentives or perks for overtime. They felt that the work environment was unchallenging and work given to them was tedious. Additionally, the trainers were made to handle departments which were beyond their job description such as stores, laundry, etc. and the supervisor expected to get weekly reports from them regarding the work they had performed in the ancillary departments assigned to them. It was very difficult for the trainers to continue with their job. Stating these reasons they started resigning and hence the Attrition rate in WCSC started to rise.

Although all the measures taken by WCSC for employee engagement and assessment were as per International standards but still the Master Trainers like Mr. Adil Ahmed were resigning from their jobs due to the ever increasing stress and tension at work after only six months of their services to the organisation.

Adil decided it was the last day at office for him, after giving a lot of thought to issues related to his career front, he had decided to resign from WCSC with immediate effect. He was learning nothing due to the work pressures from all ends and felt that the work was becoming too mechanical for his taste and moreover he was finding it next to impossible to satisfy the supervisor through his work. His career growth seems to be stagnant forever. From being a promising and exuberating trainer, he was becoming more like a mediocre employee who is performing his duty just for the sake of doing.

He was sitting in the board room along with the HR Head and Director of WCSC, explaining the reasons for his resignation. He had been waiting for this meeting for a long time. After taking a long breath he started narrating his ordeal, he mentioned the prime reasons for his resignation as extended working hours without any incentives or perks, unmanageable workload, unscrupulous work culture and biased attitude of the supervisor. He told them that the goals assigned to him were unrealistic and he was not given proper appreciation for his work in the organisation. He said that the timeline given for completing a given task was very short and due to overlapping of tasks it became very difficult to manage and complete the entire work in set deadlines which further lead to stress and embarrassment. He mentioned that there was a lack of proper leadership and the promotional opportunities were very limited. There was nothing in the job apart from the monthly remuneration. There was no medical welfare scheme in place and no provision for provident fund.

CONCLUSION

The resignations and simultaneous increase in the attrition rate of employees had opened the eyes of the management. The supervisor understood the importance and value of non-monetary motivation for the employees. Adequate measures were taken to develop positive work culture and employee relationships. Due to the aftershocks of the past situation, WCSC had lost some of its valued and promising master trainers and huge financial losses were incurred to instil new blood into the organisation.

QUESTIONS FOR DISCUSSION

1. What measures can be taken to control the attrition rate of Master Trainers?
2. How can WCSC motivate their trainers and enhance employee relationships?
3. What are the reasons which lead to a situation where Master Trainers started to resign although they were paid above par as per industry standards?
4. "Work culture" plays a more important role in employee retention as compared to financial motivation. Discuss.

REFERENCES

Armstrong, M. (2009). *Armstrong's Handbook of Human Resource Management Practice.* London: Kogan Page.

Bhatnagar, J., Puri R., Jha, H.M. (2004). Managing innovation strategic HRM: The balanced scorecard performance management system at ITC Hotels. *South Asian Journal of Management, 11(4),* 92-110.

Booth, S., and Hamer, K. (2007). Labour turnover in the retail industry: Predicting the role of individual, organisational and environmental factors, *International Journal of Retail & Distribution Management, 35(4),* 289-307.

Cheese, T. & Craig. (2008). *Engagement: The talent powered organization.* London: Kongan Page.

Education Sector in India. (2015, November). Retrieved January 5, 2016, from http://www.ibef.org/industry/education-sector-india.aspx
Murphy, E. (2009). *Coach for achievement: Talent IQ.* Platinum Press: U.S.A.

Phillips, J.J., and Connell, A.O. (2003). *Managing Employee Retention: A Strategic accountability approach.* Elsevier.

Wayne, F. and Boudreau, J. (2008). Investing in people: Financial impact of Human resource initiatives. *FT Press.* 288-293.

CHAPTER 20

Business Schools to Business Houses: Bridging the Skill Gap

EXECUTIVE SUMMARY

The Senior Human Resource Manager of 'MTC Infotech Ltd (MTCIL)' Ms. Malvika Luthra was facing an arduous task, due to the skill gaps prevailing between the current prerequisites of business personnel and the MBA postgraduates who were being recruited through the different 'Placement Drives' done from Business Schools. Malvika was also concerned about the uncertainty of the fresher's tenure in their jobs. The company was trying to retain new joinees because of increasing recruitment cost to the company. This increased attrition was causing unnecessary capital expenditure. Resultantly the organization was facing several kinds of recruitment challenges.

Operating in a competitive era where the aptitudes or skills of an employee play a vital role in development and advancement of the organization, the requirement to recruit proficient personnel is of paramount importance.

This case highlights the skill gaps arising due to inefficient training during educational programs of the candidates and the problems faced by the organizations due to their frequent attrition post recruitment.

Keywords: HR Issues in Organizations, HR Policies, Management Education, Corporate Hiring, Recruitment Process, Placement Drives, Skilled personnel

CHANCHAL SHARMA

Chanchal Sharma is an Assistant Professor at Ajay Kumar Garg Institute of Management, Ghaziabad since July, 2015. She has been working as a full time faculty in management institutions for about six years. She has received her M. Phil degree from MBU, Solan in 2011. She did her MBA from Sunderdeep Engineering College, Ghaziabad in 2010 with specialization in Human Resource (HR) and Finance. She has proficiency in subjects like Managerial Economics, Organizational Behaviour, Industrial Management and Industrial Psychology. She has published research papers in various national and international journals. She has also presented and published research papers in various conferences such as IIT, Delhi, RDIAS, New Delhi etc. She has also contributed a chapter for the book 'Innovation and Creativity Management- The Design for Future' by Makkar, Sanjeev and Jain. She has attended few workshops for various research methodologies being adopted nowadays. Her current research interests include performance appraisal, motivation, job satisfaction and organizational citizenship behaviour.

SETTING THE STAGE

Ms. Malvika Luthra was sitting in her cabin with a box of resignation letters of ex-employees stockpiled over the past three years. While she was scanning the 'Reasons to leave the organization' in the letters, she found no specific reason for this attrition. This left her completely perplexed. There was a constant pressure from the management to recruit suitable candidates who could commit to the organization for longer periods of time. She considered introduction of signing legal bonds with the new recruits to either stay with the organization for certain duration of time or face financial implications. Further, she was looking at redesigning of job description of the employees, specifically of the new recruits.

ORGANIZATIONAL BACKGROUND

Alok Srivastava was the founder of MTC Infotech Limited. He founded the company in the year 1986. The company's corporate office was situated in Greater Noida, Uttar Pradesh. The company started by five friends in a small rented premise, now stands 18,000 strong. With offices in all major Indian metros, MTCIL has also established operations all over Europe and United States.

There is an interesting story behind the conception of 'MTCIL'. In the year 1986, during the lunch hours at Delhi Garment Factory (DGF), five young and energetic technicians gathered in the office canteen. Despite having satisfactory jobs which were paying them sufficiently they were unhappy with their job profiles. At DGF, they were bound to perform the assigned tasks only but they wanted to do something more innovative and challenging. Thus, with a dream of starting their own firm they decided to quit their respective jobs, together. The person responsible for fueling the aspirations of his four other colleagues was a 31 year old technician from Bangalore, Alok Srivastava. As a result, the tech-giant that MTCIL is today was born. Alok and his four colleagues then started their journey with small, calculated steps and with time took the company to unparalleled heights.

MTCIL provided a diverse portfolio of embedded and application software together with IT consultancy, research & development, business process outsourcing and off-shore systems management. The company also offered services to various industrial sectors such as Financial Institutions, Defense Sector, Telecommunications, Retail Firms and Automobile Industry. MTCIL focused on creativity management and value creation through quality services.

MTCIL MARKET IN INDIA

MTCIL has been a recurring name in the prominent "Bloomberg Today" list and other respectable publications. This acknowledgement further distinguished the company from various others of the field, which had a market capitalization of $3 billion or more. It was one of the largest public dealing organizations in India. Therefore, MTCIL was considered to be one of the best companies to work in. MTCIL now had total staff strength of 18,000 worldwide.

The given quantitative data and market value of the firm shows the competitiveness of the organization which was at stake due to the emerging problems within the organization.

CASE DESCRIPTION

Malvika Luthra, the Senior Human Resource (HR) Manager of MTCIL, was confronted with various critical issues like high churn rate of recently recruited personnel and lack of desired skill-set needed by the organization. Initially, the company was striving to retain new employees within the organization so as to reduce the operational cost incurred in the recruitment process. The company's fundamental principle was 'Hire-to-Retire' to manage big asset portfolios and ensure competence and effectiveness. Earlier the company had focused on hiring staff with sharp minds and fresh talent to give a new perspective to the system. With the passage of time this practice discontinued and the pattern had now changed due to high attrition and unavailability of suitable talent in the market.

In order to solve the problems, Malvika went for a recruitment drive to a Business School in New Delhi. The project teams were looking for candidates with prior work experience because they were facing problems with frequent exit of fresh graduates selected in the recent recruitment drives. The fresh entrants who were appointed or recruited in the organization through various recruitment drives were inconsistent with their tenures in the organization, thus creating a detrimental effect in two ways. Firstly, it was increasing the cost of recruitment to the company and secondly, causing loss of goodwill of the company. Furthermore, Malvika was also facing problems with the constant unsatisfactory feedback of the skill-set of the new recruits by the team heads. For effective and timely delivery of the ongoing projects, the need of current recruits to keep working on the projects was a mandatory criterion.

Being the Senior HR Manager, Malvika traditionally liked to recruit pass-outs with minimal experience on economically favorable packages earlier but now she had asked her team members to get experienced candidates with work experience and yet ensure that the company did not over-pay for them.

As the reasons for instability of the employees in the organization are attributed to 'Incompetent Management', it was a point of concern for both the Management and HR department of the company. The management of MTCIL had asked the HR Team to conduct a survey among the team heads in order to analyze the reasons behind the attrition of the new joinees. The recommendations of this survey pointed towards the lack of sincerity among fresh entrants with respect to their jobs and several other startling revelations.

ORGANIZATIONAL CHALLENGES

Malvika was faced with a dilemma of whether to align with the older strategies and methodologies of staffing the personnel or to change the base eligibility criteria from fresh graduates to graduates with at least one year of job experience. Further, in sync with problems of the organization, Malvika tried to highlight the shortcomings of the prevailing business education system with respect to what the large business houses are searching for in their employees.

There was a need to identify the development and improvement of the MBA program which commenced during the "Corporate Based Era" of the 1900s to in order to narrow the gap between Business Schools and Business Houses.

WAY FORWARD

In order to find possible solutions to the issue, the Human Resource Team of MTCIL was tasked with conducting a survey of different B-Schools of National Capital Region (NCR) specifically with the objective to review the professional courses being taught to the students. The HR Team formulated and conducted 'Educational Institutions Survey-2015'. The recommendations of the survey highlighted the wide gap existing between - what is being taught at the business schools and the skills and abilities that are demanded by the organization for sustained development.

The results of survey pointed out that in the current scenario, business schools are only teaching the students theoretical knowledge. Therefore, to get skilled candidates who have the finest intellectual capability again becomes a point of consideration. There is a lack of practical methodologies in the pedagogy and also a need to keep pace with the changing era in a globalized world.

Moral values like sincerity and honesty should be inculcated in the students which may make them loyal towards their organizations. Also, they should be internally as well as externally be motivated towards their jobs.

RECOMMENDATIONS

After analysing the results of the survey, few significant decisions were taken by Malvika with respect to the recruitment process to be followed by the organization. She focused on applying 'Buy Decision Strategy' of the recruitment process instead of 'Make Decision Strategy'. Buy decision strategy refers to the recruitment of experienced and skilled candidates rather than hiring fresh graduates who lacked KSA i.e. knowledge, skills and aptitude with respect to a specific job.

The survey reviews further paved the way for various Institutions/Colleges of NCR to incorporate various initiatives in order to increase the effectiveness and potential of freshers which may result in possible hiring of the students. Post the survey, Management of the institutions gave serious consideration to this issue. The administrative counsellors tried to find out the reasons and areas where there were lacunae. The educationists pointed out certain measures in order to overcome the observed problems:

- Earlier only theoretical knowledge was being imparted to the students. Therefore, in order to use advanced methodologies, learning through behavioural sciences was adopted. Behavioural science helped in better understanding management concepts by practically employing them in a situation. It served the purpose of inculcating practical knowledge in the students.
- In order to instill the required skill set in postgraduates, training of students in skill laboratories also became a part of their pedagogy. Various simulations and finance labs were introduced. The simulation labs allow teaching causal theoretical concepts to the students in a risk free environment. Students acquire

the desired set of skills by demonstrating competence and excellence. Towards the growing trend of realism, simulation lab is completely a new approach of teaching.

- In order to gain experiential learning, applying real-time research, analysing organizations, observing and interfacing with the market in a factitious environment, generating investment ideas etc.; financial labs are the best examples. These labs also provide a trading floor for the post graduates.

Various transformations were done by the institutions regarding the practical implications of various educational modules, in order to align with the competitiveness and intensity demanded in the jobs by various industries. Since, faculty members are responsible for inculcating values and qualities in the students, therefore in order to serve this purpose Faculty Development Program (FDP) became a part of the faculty curriculum. It further allowed the Institutions to start various advanced programs for them in B-Schools with respect to amended educational modules and course pattern being adopted. Apart from organizing FDP's in different institutions of NCR, some distinctive case teaching workshops or workshops on pedagogy were also incorporated.

QUESTIONS FOR DISCUSSION

1. What are the issues and challenges existing in management education?
2. What are the traits that corporate recruiters seek in fresh MBA entrants?
3. What points should be kept in mind while constructing a management training module?
4. What are the ways to hone the students with the optimum skills and aptitude in such a manner that they are worthy for the prospective recruiters?

REFERENCES

Bersin, J. (2012, 10 December). *Growing Gap Between What Business Needs and What Education Provides.*
Retrieved January 31, 2016, from
http://www.forbes.com/sites/joshbersin/2012/12/10/growing-gap-between-what-business-needs-and-what-education-provides/#d2d71b876bf1
Bridging the Gap between Education and the Workplace: Equipping People with the Right Skills for Today and Tomorrow's Jobs. (2015, 15 May)
Retrieved February 20, 2016, from
http://www.accaglobal.com/lk/en/discover/news/2015/05/education-workplace.html

Mehra, L. (n.d.). *Bridging the skills gap with industry: Academia partnerships.*
Retrieved January 31, 2016, from
http://www.cisco.com/web/IN/about/network/academia_partnerships.html

Morparia, K. (2016, 13 January). *Bridging The Gap Between Education And Employment.*
Retrieved February 20, 2016, from
http://businessworld.in/article/Bridging-The-Gap-Between-Education-And-Employment/13-01-2016-90214/

ABOUT THE AUTHORS

Dr. Anupama Rajesh
Associate Professor
Head – T&D, MDP and Consultancy
Amity Business School, Amity University, India

Her qualifications include PhD in the area of Technology in Education, M.Phil. (IT), M.Phil. (Mgmt.), M.Ed., M.Sc. (IT), PGDCA, PGDBA. She has a teaching experience of about 20 years including international assignments which include a teaching stint at Singapore and training of Italian and French delegates and students. She has written more than 20 research papers and case studies for prestigious international journals and has three books and several book chapters to her credit. She is reviewer of renowned Sage and Emerald journals and is the Editor of "Anukriti" - The Amity Business School Magazine. Her research interests are Business Intelligence, Educational Technology, marketing analytics etc. while her teaching interests are Business Intelligence, E-Commerce and IT enabled processes.

She is an avid trainer and has trained Union Bank of India, NHPC, ILFS, TATA Motors, Bhutan Power Company employees as well as Commonwealth Games Volunteers and army personnel. She is a Master Trainer from Microsoft and an Infosys Partner for Business Intelligence.

She is Head – Training, Development & Consultancy; and Area Head (IT) for Management and Head of the Executive MBA Programme at Amity Business School, Amity University, India.

She has won the ADMA Research Award. She has also been awarded "Shiksha Rattan Puruskar" by IIF Society and won the second "Best Paper Award" at IIM Ahmedabad. She recently presented a case study at INSEAD Paris. She also has a MOOC to her credit.

http://amitymooc.com/home/itm.php

Prateek Mangal

Prateek works as the Director – Client Services for SSR Management Consultants Pvt. Ltd. An MBA from Indian Institute of Foreign Trade, Kolkata and International University in Geneva, Switzerland, he started his corporate journey with Triton Management Services and served the FMCG giant in Africa and India. He is widely travelled and experienced across Europe, Africa and Asia and has six year of experience in FMCG and Manufacturing Industry.

He has a passion to gather knowledge and is also a Diploma holder in Cyber Law from Asian School of Cyber Laws, Pune. He has also been part of numerous Conclaves and Symposiums and has presented and published research papers on key FMCG and Manufacturing issues.

Prateek is a prominent Social Worker as well and runs an NGO 'Neelabh Foundation' to finance studies of underprivileged children in eastern Uttar Pradesh.

NIRAV SAHNI

Nirav is pursuing a Bachelor of Commerce in Finance and Marketing at McGill University in Canada. He has corporate experience from interning at Deloitte in their Financial Advisory Department and has also interned at Sanghavi Diamonds. A keen entrepreneur, Nirav is active in the start-up community currently working on an e-commerce and big data venture: VRentin where he holds the position of the Chief Business Officer. Prior to McGill, Nirav has taken courses in Financial Statistics and Economics at Harvard University where he was ranked amongst the top 5% of his class. An avid learner with interest in Emerging Markets, he has attended conferences at Harvard Business School and Columbia Business School. He has been awarded the Principal's Medal for Excellence in Academics and has also been a state level swimmer in India. He is actively involved in the student community at university and is also a part of the student government. His most recent publication is a case study on the Co-operative Dairy sector in Gujarat that was published by the Case Centre, UK.

Printed in the United States
By Bookmasters